MULLUKURUMBA
RE-VISITED

MULLUKURUMBA
RE-VISITED

B. ANANDA BHANU
SEETHA KAKKOTH

SERIALS PUBLICATIONS
NEW DELHI (INDIA)

First Published - 2007

ISBN : 978-81-8387-107-5

Published by

SERIALS PUBLICATIONS
4830/24, Prahlad Street, Ansari Road
Darya Ganj, New Delhi-110002 (India)
Phone : 23245225. Fax : 91-11-23272135
E-mail: serials@satyam.net.in

To the Memory

of

Smt. Rajalakshmi Misra

CONTENTS

FOREWORD

The first ever known references such as Dravir and Asuras in the Mahabharatha, the greatest and the longest epic of all times, were made probably about the ancestors of the tribes of today. The British not only considered the study of the tribes of India as adventurous but fascinating too. The anthropologists of India have altered this approach since India's independence. For an alien population, of course, the study of the tribes of India was adventurous and fascinating, but for the Indians, it was a necessity, an obligation, a constitutional prerogative to identify and recognize the tribes of India as part of our own culture and civilization so as to help them lead a cheerful and comfortable life.

Dr. B. Ananda Bhanu, Professor and Head of the Department of Anthropology, Kannur University, along with his colleague Dr. Seetha Kakkoth, is presenting us with a precious book on one of the tribes of Nilgiri-Wayanad under the title Mullukurumba Revisited. The book is the outcome of several years of enormous research experience on the tribes of South India. Kannur University is proud of this contribution, which is a result of prolonged and genuine research talents. The book is written in simple language, and is free from technical jargons. The style of narration is not only critical but informative as well. By publishing this Monograph under the Monograph Series, Professor Bhanu and his colleague Dr. Seetha Kakkoth have upheld the intellectual tradition initiated by Dr. A. Aiyappan, the world renowned anthropologist of Kerala and the former Vice-Chancellor of Kerala University. I had the opportunity of listening to the scholarly speeches of Dr. Aiyappan while I was doing my graduation in the University College, Trivandrum. The authors of this book have taken a lot of care to present us authentic data and meaningful generalizations.

Dr. P. Chandramohan
Vice-Chancellor

PREFACE

For centuries, the tribes of India have been in contact with the societies living around them. The culture contact thus resulted in reciprocal borrowing of cultural elements, influenced the life-style of the tribes more than the non-tribes, who were in continuous contact. However, the nature of culture contact and interaction with their neighbouring dominant populations, both castes and communities, was distinctively different from place to place. The tribes of southern India exhibit maximum cultural changeability when compared to the castes and communities. This is mainly because of the presence of Western Ghats, which separates the southern states from the rest of the country, particularly Kerala from Karnataka and Tamil Nadu. The Western and Eastern slopes as a result of the meeting of Western Ghats with Eastern Ghats and the evergreen rain forest still restrict its inhabitants from free and frequent cultural interaction and 'integration' with each other. Cultural elements of the dominant Hindu castes are being adopted by the tribal cultures due to their prolonged and direct cultural contact and interaction. The tribes living in the interior of forests and leading hunting and gathering life are still away from such interaction, 'integration' and 'assimilation'.

The Mullukurumba, being an agricultural tribe, are in continuous contact with their neighbours since centuries, and this contact condition has led them to adopt or accept many cultural elements from the dominant Hindus living around them. This occurred due to the fact that the Mullukurumba happened to be technologically primitive and economically backward or weaker compared to the migrant populations particularly the Chettis, Nairs, Christians and Muslims.

The main aim of publication of this ethnographic account in the form of a monograph under the title "Mullukurumba Revisited" is to analyze the nature of culture change or acculturation among the Mullukurumba of Nilgiri–Wayanad. The contact situation has been examined, analyzed, compared and generalized. An attempt has been made to evolve a model of social or culture change among the Mullukurumba. This model has been presented, interpreted and theorized in this book as an adaptive strategy of the Mullukurumba to cope up with the changing situations and challenging opportunities emerging around them due to mass migration of settlers from the plains, cash crop cultivation, urbanization, modernization of communication network, implementation of development programmes by various agencies and development of townships.

The first monograph on the Mullukurumba was written by Rajalakshmi Misra and published by the Anthropological Survey of India in 1971. Therefore, a restudy after 35 years is an essential prerequisite to understand the nature of social and cultural change and the mode of transformation taking place among the Mullukurumba. My association with Dr. P.K. Misra (Regional Officer Anthropological Survey of India, Government of India, Southern Regional Circle, Mysore) and his wife Smt. Rajalakshmi Misra (Assistant Anthropologist, Anthropological Survey of India, Government of India, Southern Regional Circle, Mysore), since my employment in the Anthropological Survey of India, Government of India, Southern Regional Circle, Mysore in 1977 and as a Lecturer in Cultural Anthropology, Tribal Research Centre, Tamil University, Uthagamandalam in 1984 helped and steered my thinking and influenced my academic growth. My wife and me loved them and treated them like our own parents. We enjoyed their love and affections and hospitality more than anybody else in the Anthropological Survey of India, Mysore and Tribal Research Centre, Tamil University then. I owe them my intellectual debt as my teachers and supervisors. I am dedicating this book in memory of late Smt. Rajalakshmi Misra from whom I learnt the basic qualities to become a good researcher.

My first visit to the Mullukurumba settlements was in 1976 while I was working as Senior Research Fellow, Tribal Research Centre (present KIRTADS), Kozhikode. I stayed in Karumam (Pulpally, Wayanad) for more than six months in two spells of three months duration, while I was conducting an ethnographic study on the Kattunayakans of Pulpally. To visit some of the Kattunayakan settlements I had to cross the settlements of Mullukurumba regularly. I visited the house of late Sri. Raghavan Master, former M.L.A., a member of the Mullukurumba tribe of Pulpally, several occasions. Late Sri. Raghavan Master, M.L.A. and late Sri Rajan Master former M.L.A. (a member of the Adiyan tribe of Mananthawady) were my close friends and visited me while I was working among the Cholanaickan of Nilambur in 1975. I also remember the help extended to me by Dr. P.R.G. Mathur, the then Special Officer, Tribal Research and Training Centre, Kozhikode and Sri T. Mathava Menon, the then Director, Tribal Welfare and Special Secretary to Government of Kerala. I am thankful to all of them for their help and encouragement during the tenure of my fellowship and thereafter. While working in the Anthropological Survey of India, Mysore, I had several occasions to visit the tribes of Nilgiri–Wayanad. Of my several visits to the Mullukurumba, the most important one was when I accompanied late Smt. Rajalakshmi Misra and an Ambassador (from Japan), who visited the Anthropological Survey of India, Mysore in 1978. I also visited the Mullukurumba of Kappala and the tribal areas of Wayanad along with Sri. Ashok Tiwari, Museum Curator, and Sri. Francis Kulirani, Senior Technical Assistant of the Anthropological Survey of India, Mysore in connection with the collection of artifacts from the tribal areas of Nilgiris and Kerala in 1980. I extend my sincere thanks to Sri. Tiwari, Dr. Francis Kulirani and Sri Ramaswamy, Driver, for making the field trip and collection of artifacts possible within the time schedule. My third visit to the settlement of Mullukurumbas of Kappala was when Dr. P.K. Misra joined the Department of Anthropology as Professor of Anthropology, University of Mysore in 1981. He had asked me to accompany the Faculty members who were taking the Post-Graduate Students of the Department of Anthropology, University of Mysore to Kappala. The faculty members were not familiar with the tribal terrain in Nilgiri–Wayanad. I owe my debt of gratitude to all of them who were with me then.

While working as Lecturer in Cultural Anthropology, Tribal Research Centre, Tamil University, Uthagamandalam, I stayed in Kappala close to the Mullukurumba settlement for a month in 1985. I was collecting data for the 'Evaluation of the Rehabilitation of the Paniya Bonded Labourers' in Kappala adjacent to the settlement of the Mullukurumba. Later on when I joined the Department of Anthropology, University of Calicut as Senior Lecturer, I had arranged a fieldwork for one month among the Mullukurumba of Nilgiri – Wayanad in 1990. Twelve Post-graduate students of the Department of Anthropology, University of Calicut were taken to the field and stayed in Kappala settlement for one month. During this time I could visit some of the settlements of Mullukurumba of Sulthan Battery. Dr. Vineetha Menon, Lecturer and Head of the Department of Anthropology, University of Calicut supervised the fieldwork during the second half of 15 days. I have pleasure in acknowledging the help and assistance extended to me by my colleagues and the first batch of students of the Department of Anthropology particularly to Sri. Babu Ambalaparambath, Sri. George Tharakan, Sri. Harischandran, Smt. Bindu Balakrishnan, Smt. Jessy Joseph, P., Smt. Laly Francis K., Smt. Leena, P.L., Smt. Vidya Chandrasekhar, Sri. Satheesan Alakkadan, Sri Prasanth, Sri. Premarajan, K and Smt. Deepthi Mary Jacob. However, the data collected then were not enough to write a monograph of this kind. Generalization and model building were done recently based on my revisits and collection of additional data, which were subjected to re–examination and further testing and analysis for new interpretations.

I owe my debt of gratitude to the Vice–Chancellor and Registrar, University of Calicut for giving financial assistance to conduct fieldwork among the Mullukurumba of Nilgiri–Wayanad during 1990 and for other subsequent field visits and study tours organized by the Departments since the inception of the Department of Anthropology in the University of Calicut. I am also thankful to the Vice–Chancellor and the Registrar, Kannur University for extending financial support for organizing fieldwork and study tours to the tribal areas of Nilgiri–Wayanad since 1997.

I owe special debt of gratitude to the leaders of the Mullukurumba of Nilgiri–Wayanad for extending hospitality and supporting us with valuable data without which this book would not have been possible.

I have had fruitful discussions with Dr. Seetha Kakkoth, my student colleague of the Department of Anthropology since her joining as Field Assistant in December 2003. She had worked for several months to modify the earlier draft of the manuscript and made extensive comments. Considering the constant endeavor she had put in to re-assemble a large body of data and convert them into a readable book form, I have immense pleasure in making her a co-author of this book.

I am immensely grateful to Dr. Chandramohan, Vice–Chancellor of Kannur University for sparing his valuable time to read the manuscript and writing a foreword to this book and making it more meaningful, memorable and acceptable to both the academics and the general public.

I express my sincere thanks to Dr. S. Josh, Reader, Department of Studies in English, Kannur University for his encouragement and valuable suggestions.

Last, but not the least, I must place on record my special sense of gratitude to the Serials Publications, New Delhi for undertaking the enormous job of printing and publishing this book within a short span of time.

B. ANANDA BHANU

Chapter - 1

INTRODUCTION

THE TRIBES OF INDIA AND THEIR HISTORY

The experts on the tribes of India are of the view that the ancestors of the present tribes of India were the first inhabitants in this continent (Baine 1891 Risley 1901; 1905, Grigson 1931). The names such as *adivasi, adimjati* etc clearly convey the fact that they came first (*adi* = earliest or first and *vasi* = inhabitants). Recent interpretations on peopling of India based on archaeological, anthropological and linguistic data support this. Till the last phase of 20th Century, we believed that the *Nishadas* (Austro-Asiatic Family of Languages) came to India through Middle East 30,000 years B.P. They first came to middle India and moved to the Himalayas and adjacent areas. Majority of the tribal languages spoken in this region even today fall under the language family *Nishada*. The second migration was that of the *Kiratas* (Tibato–Chinese Family of Languages). The term *Kirata* had been used then for the non–Aryans (Chatterji 1968). The *Dravidians* (Dravidian family of languages) also came along with the *Kiratas*. The period of migration of these two groups is estimated as 8000–10,000 years B.P. The *Kiratas* after reaching Central India moved towards North-Eastern India and reached Tibet and then China and adjacent areas. The *Kiratas* are also known as Sino-Tibetan

Family of Language speakers. This shows a second return migration from China to Tibet. The *Dravidians* inhabited the middle India including the Deccan plains and the adjacent regions and reached even the valleys and highlands of *Vindya* (Hewitt 1888: 89) and the *Sindh* (Pathak 1972 cf. Vidyarthi and Rai 1985). We have no hesitation to say that the people who inhabited the banks of the submerged river *Saraswathy* were the *Dravidians*. The third group of migration was that of the *Aryans* (Indo-European Family of language speakers) who came just 4000–6000 years B.P. Max Muller (1887) estimates the antiquity of Vedic literature as just 1200–1000 B.C.

The *Aryans* who came with a script and sharp iron weapons were technologically advanced compared to the other three groups who came earlier and settled here. Technological superiority and the use of horse for movement could dominate the earlier inhabitants, and therefore, the *Dravidians* were pushed down to the south beyond Deccan plateau. According to Leuva (1963) there are clear indications in the *Vedas* and *Puranas* including the *Manu samhitas* that 'some of the earlier inhabitants were defeated and outcasted'. Vyas (1967: 24–43) argues that the term like *Rakshasa*, *Asura* referred to in the Ramayana are nothing but the earlier inhabitants of India.

The theory suggested above i.e., the migration of the four major language groups, was accepted by most of the scholars in the field of Linguistics, Archaeology and Anthropology. The earlier interpretations of the Anthropologists based on the racial categories became meaningless in the light of more valid and scientific data and interpretations based on comparison. The interdisciplinary approach used by the scientists particularly the Linguistic classification, Archaeological interpretations based on the findings from the above regions, and anthropological data generated by the Anthropological Survey of India through the National Project on 'People of India' became a landmark in the reconstruction of the cultural history of India.

The recent finding of a fossil near Pondicherry–'Laterite baby'–by Rajendran (2003), an archaeologist, has been dated as old as 1.66 lakh years. DNA molecular analysis of the blood of the Jenukuruba, a Dravidian tribe of Karnataka, by the scientists of the Anthropological Survey of India, Mysore (personal communication) establishes that the ancestors of the Jenukurubas of Karnataka had reached India probably 85,000 years B.P. The fossil finding of Rajendran (2003), which is the second oldest fossil unearthed in India, and the interpretations of this fossil by Rajendran and others (2003, 2004, 2006), clarly take the antiquity of human beings in the southern part of India as early as 1.7 lakh years. This finding reaffirms the fact that there was a migration through the sea from South Africa to Southern India before 1,00,000 years B.P. There is a gap of 55,000 years or more between the *Nishada* and the present findings. Thus, the argument such as the first 'migration through the sea route' seems to be scientifically valid and acceptable to anthropologists compared to the earlier interpretations supporting the 'migration through land route'. The earlier interpretation also is correct, but it is applicable only to those who came later, say 30,000 years B.P., through a land route, particularly for the *Nishadas,* followed by the *Kiratas* and not for the *Dravidians.*

Thus, the current thinking is that the *Dravidians*, representing the simplest food gathering tribes of South India today, including the Jenukuruba, Cholanaickan, Kattunayakan, Paniyan, Adiyan, Uralikuruman, Mullukurumba, Kadar, Aranadan, Irular and other similar groups are the direct descendants of the earliest inhabitants of India. Writers on the subject held similar arguments earlier too (e.g. Lacey 1931:272, Shoobert 1931:312). The heterogeneity or cultural variation that we see among these *Dravidian* tribes as well as among the *Dravidian* language speakers today is due to their contact, intra and inter interactions with their neighbours during the course of their existence as argued by Baine (1891:118), Risley (1901:98), O'Malley (1911:235), Shoobert (1931:403), Ghurye (1963:12) and Bose (1971).

These being the facts, some of the writers on the history of the peopling of India mixed up the linguistic categories with racial classifications and prolonged the discussions and created confusions among the scholars. Writings on the Negroid and Mongoloid elements on the Indian populations by Dalton (1872), Hutton (1921; 1923), Guha (1935; 1944), Majumdar (1961), Elwin (1955:33), Aiyappan (1936; 1937; 1948) and Dube (1969:62) opened up new areas for further arguments and criticisms. While writing on the early ethno-history of India Aiyappan (1988:13) argues, "India began with a small negritoid population, which used only very primitive natural tools, and if they made any stone tools, they were of simplest order. These Negritoes have almost disappeared as a pure strain, but still survive in an infinitesimal degree in the hills of the Western Ghats, particularly the Kadar tribe of the Anamalai Hills, its chief recognizable character being shortness of stature and thin almost wooly hair, which shows a flat cross-section when examined under the microscope. .... T.H. Huxley was the first biologist to recognize this racial strain, which is now generally known as Proto-Australoid". Thus the arguments went out of track for several years, and thus the linguistic classifications remained underground all these years.

RESEARCH ON THE TRIBES OF SOUTH INDIA

British administrators and Anthropologists started research on the tribes of South India since colonial period. The British gave first priority to the general administration of India including the tribal areas. A few eminent Indian anthropologists too have made their own contributions in the area of tribal research. This resulted in the publication of a few good ethnographic reports, monographs on the tribes of South India by British administrators turned anthropologists and Indian scholars. The monographs and a few articles that have become the landmarks in the field of ethnography are the Todas of Nilgiris (Rivers 1906; Anthony Walker 1986), Castes and Tribes of Southern India (Thurston 1909), Tribes and Castes of Madras Presidency (Sherring

1909), Kota (Mandelbaum 1938; 1941; 1970, Verghese 1974), Chenchus (Haimendorf 1943), Mysore Tribes and Castes (Ananthakrishna Iyer, L.K. 1908; 1912; 1928–1935), The Travancore Tribes and Castes (Krishna Iyer L.A. 1937– 1941; 1961), Kadar of Cochin (Ehrenfels 1941; 1952), Kanikkars of Travancore (Bhabananda Mukherjee 1953; 1956; Gnanambal 1954; Nag 1954; Ray 1955), Malapantarams (Bhabananda Mukherjee 1954; Brain Morris 1976; 1977), Tribes of Kerala (Luiz 1962), Yanadis (Raghaviah 1956; 1962), Badaga (Paul Hockings 1965), Jenu Kuruba (Misra 1969), Mullu Kurumba (Rajalakshmi Misra 1971), Palleyan (Gardiner1972), Soliga (Morab 1977), Tribal Situation in Kerala (Mathur 1977), Hakki Pikki (Mann 1980), Cholanaickan of Kerala (Bhanu 1989) and Dravidian Tribes (Menon and Sasikumar 1999).

The National Project on the People of India launched under the leadership of K.S. Singh in 1986 has resulted in the publication of 43 volumes under the National and State series. The tribes of India have been discussed in these volumes along with other castes and tribes. Three separate volumes giving abstracts on all communities are also included in these publications (Singh 1999). The publication of these volumes is considered as a landmark in the history of research on the People of India after India's independence. Compared to the earlier volume on The People of India by Risley (1905), these 43 volumes give a full understanding on the nature of Indian Caste System, Scheduled Castes and Scheduled Tribes and Communities such as the Christians and the Muslims. These publications made research on the Castes and Tribes of India more meaningful and systematic. The use of secondary data and data generated by field investigators spending just two to three days in the field for recording changes since the publication of the monograph on the group under study, made it synchronic.

A brief ethnography on the Mullukurumba is given in the State volume on People of India, Kerala State (Singh 2002). The ethnographic details included in this volume are based on the earlier publications starting from Thurston

(1909) to Rajalakshmi Misra (1971). Although the monograph on Mullukurumba appeared in 1971, the fieldwork for the collection of data for the write up of this monograph was done much earlier, and therefore, we felt to have a restudy on the Mullukurumba so as to bring out another publication in the form of a monograph describing their lifestyle including the changes since the publication of the first monograph, which is taken as the base line data. Data on the Mullukurumbas of Wayanad, Kerala, have also been included in this volume so as to get a complete picture of the Mullukurumba spread over in two States namely Tamil Nadu (Nilgiris) and Kerala (Wayanad). This is done for the reason that there is only one group of tribe under the name Mullukurumba, who happened to be in two States due to the reorganization of the state boundaries (Luiz 1962; Tharakan and Bhanu1994; Sasikumar 1999; Bindu 2006).

According to the Census of India 2001, the total tribal population in Wayanad was 1,36,062 (28,373 in Nilgiris), which probably includes the Mullukurumba population too, although the prefix in the name *mullu* is not seen recorded in any of the Census operations so far. What is recorded in the Census of India is the term Kurumbas, who are found only in the Attappady (Palakkad district). In Wayanad there are two types of 'Kurumbas' with a prefix such as Mullukurumba and Uralikuruman. Separate population figure for Mullukurumba is not available, since the Government of India included the Mullukurumba and Bettakurumbas (Uralikuruman) in one category i.e., Kurumans. However, as per the Scheduled Castes and Scheduled Tribes Orders (Amendment) Act, 2002 (Act 10 OF 2003) Vide Part-VII–Kerala–Second Schedule notified in the Gazette of India dated 8-1-2002, the Mullukurumba were added along with Kurumans (Serial No.17) as Mulla Kuruman, Mullu Kuruman and Mala Kuruman.

Etymologically, the term *mullu* means thorn and *kurumba* means mischief. Thus, the word Mullukurumba means mischief thorn makers. According to Thurston (1909) the Kurumbas or Kurubas are the modern representatives of the ancient Kurumbas or Pallavas, who were once so powerful throughout southern India. The Chola King Adoadai about the seventh or eighth century A.D affected the final overthrow of the Kurumba sovereignty and the Kurumbas were scattered far and wide. Many fled to the hills and in the Nilgiris and the Wynad, in Coorg and Mysore; representatives of this ancient race are now found as wild and uncivilized tribes.

Luiz (1962:198) sets aside the possibility of the Mullukurumbas being the modern representatives of ancient Kurumbas or the Pallavas, but agrees with the claim of the Mullukurumbas that they are the *Vedas* (*Vedans*) of South India, who after coming into Malabar were called Kurumans.

According to Aiyappan (1948:95) the Mullukurumbas are experts in hunting, and they are able to aim good shots with their bows and arrows. During the Kottayam Rajas rebellion against the Brititsh, the Mullukurumbas fought very valiantly on the side of Raja.

Rajalakshmi Misra (1971:5) narrates a myth relating to God Shiva and Goddess Parvathi. According to this myth, God Shiva and Goddess Parvathi descended on earth in the guise of hunter to grant Arjuna, the epic hero, the boon *pasupathastoram* (a special bow and arrow). The Mullukurumba further believe that God Shiva created a band of hunters to accompany him and Goddess Parvathi at that time, and that the descendants of those hunters are now known as the Mullukurumbas.

In appearance, the Mullukurumba are of light brown to dark brown complexion. Their average height is roughly between 5 and 5'6 feet. The middle aged people, both men and women look to be healthy and strong. The women look more attractive in their traditional dress. Their dialect is a mixture of Tamil and Malayalam languages. They are well versed in Malayalam and many of them are multilingual.

METHODOLOGY

The data presented in this monograph were collected from the Mullukurumba residing at Cherangod and Erumad villages in Gudallur taluk of Nilgiri District, Tamil Nadu and a few settlements in Kalpetta and Sultan Bathery of Wayanad district of Kerala State in 1990. The areas were re-visited for a couple of days every year since 1991 and in April 2006 and studied the changes since the earlier visits.

Major anthropological methods employed for data collection were observation, interview and genealogical method. Participant observation combined with interviews was the main method of collecting information. Questions were asked directly and recorded their responses briefly then and there and elaborated the details later on in the camp. There was no ambiguity with regard to the responses, since their dialect was similar to the Malayalam spoken language in the Travancore area.

A sample survey was conducted among 100 households, covering more than 60% of Mullukurumba households in Gudalur Taluk. The survey was restricted to 100 households because of time limitations. This sample survey helped in gathering quantitative data such as general information on age, sex, marital status, occupations etc. Apart from these, available documents including the monograph on Mullukurumba by Rajalakshmi Misra (1971) and several papers published on them by other researchers were also consulted.

CHAPTERISATION

This monograph is arranged in the following manner. The first chapter- Introduction–gives a brief account of the history of tribes, review of research publication of the tribes of South India, etymology and methodology. The second chapter titled 'Habitat' describes the area of study, rainfall, topography, settlement pattern, house types, material culture, food habits etc. Economic oragnisation is described in the third chapter– 'Economy'. The fourth chapter, 'Society' describes socio-political and religious organisations. 'Social Changes' occurred in this community is given in chapter–Five; and the Sixth chapter under the title 'Discussion', analysis, comparisons, generalizations and theory building are made.

Chapter - 2

HABITAT

THE SETTING

The Mullukurumbas are distributed within a radius of 30 kilometers including the eastern part of Wayanad district of Kerala State and the western part of Gudallur taluk of Nilgiri district of Tamil Nadu. These two districts of South India are known for their tribal concentration, which is unique in the country.

The Nilgiris attract researchers and foreign tourists due to its blue mountains of high altitude, cool climate, heavy rainfall and topography. The climate of Nilgiris promotes growth of rain forest, evergreen juncles and jaint grass meadows crammed with various kinds of flowers and vegetation. The average elevation of high ranges is of 6500 feet from the Mean Sea Level. The Todas, Irulars, Kurumbas, and Kotas were the earlier inhabitants in this region. The Mullukurumba live on the lower western slope of Nilgiris particularly in Gudallur upto an attitude of 3,000 feet above MSL. Gudallur taluk alone has 50% of the tribal population in Nilgiri district.

Like Nilgiris, Wayanad too is equally famous for its natural beauty and tribal population. Presence of high hills and valleys, mighty rivers and streams, meadows and paddy fields between the hills earned its name Wayanad (*wayal* means paddy field and *nadu* means an area demarcated and owned by its inhabitants). The Wayanad taluk is geographically a part of the Nilgiri Plateau. Kanarese-speaking tribes and the Western Ghats by Malayalam speaking tribes inhabit the extreme Eastern Ghats of Wayanad contiguous with the Nilgiris and Coorg. When the Nilgiri–Wayanad Plateau began to be opened by European planters, they found the country in the possession of a few landlords, chiefly Malayalees, for the whole of Wayanad area, until its cession to the East India Company by Tippu Sultan was part of the dominions of the Raja of Kottayam. The actual cultivators were the tribes, such as the Kurichiyas, Mullukurumbas and Chettis. Wayanad was invaded by Tippu Sultan of Mysore and followed by the British earlier. Establishment of foreign rule ruined the societal harmony existed then among various 'indegenous' populations including the tribes. This led to a situation where the 'sons of soil', the tribes, have been pushed down into the interior hills and valleys by the non-tribal inmigrants from southern Kerala belonging to Christian and Muslim Communities, who were in majority, and the upper caste Hindus. The habitat of the Mullukurumbas extends from the eastern part of Wayanad to the western part of Gudallur taluk. The entire habitat of the Mullukurumba is divided into four regions such as *kara nadu*, *kallu nadu*, *pakka nadu* and *naria nadu*.

The topography of these two regions (Wayanad and Gudallur) is the same, since it is nothing but an extension of the Deccan plateau, and the Mullukurumbas, who are spread over in these two regions also consider themselves as one endogamous group. The overall slope of the region is from west to east in Wayanad, and from north to south in Gudallur. The river Kabini, a tributary of the Kaveri, benefits Wayanad and Gudallur forms the head waters region of the Pandiar–Punnapuzha system flowing south and west, to join one of the mighty rivers of Kerala, the Chaliyar (Menon 1999:276).

The soil in these areas is fertile due to the decay of natural bush, and the colour of it varies from red to dark brown, and is mostly red loam mixed with laterite. In the low lying areas between hill tracks and valleys, paddy is cultivated; and on the sloppy lands a variety of cash crops like coffee, pepper, ginger and tea are planted.

Gudallur and Wayanad receive heavy rainfall during the south-west monsoon and moderate precipitation of dampness during the north-east monsoon. Stunning chill climate with occasional rainfall is experienced during December to March. The winters are extremely breezy, cool and pleasing, since the high hill ranges and higher peaks are roofed with snowfall and marvelous milky-white frost.

The whole area was once covered with natural evergreen and moist deciduos forests all around and grasslands on the higher altitudes, particularly on the peaks. But now, due to overexploitation of sandal and bamboo, the forests have crumpled. Natural forests have been converted to teak and eucalyptus plantations in the Reserve forests and tea, coffee, pepper and other commercial crops are grown in the rest of the areas. The land use pattern has tremendously been altered with the intrusion of inmigrants to this area. The wild life population too has been badly affected. Elephants, tigers and bisons have lost their original home and now they are occasionally rambling out into the plantations of inmigrants and causing concern for the 'new owners' of the forests. Lion-tailed monkeys, Nilgiri langurs, baboons, rabbits, porcupines, wild goats, various kinds of pigs, black deers, dotted deers, lizards and a variety of small and big birds are still found in the interior forests. Many of these species have become prey to the greedy poachers and hungry hunters. Powerful, wealthy, civilized and influencial predators from the plains are still recklessly roaming day and night through out the Nilgiri-Wayanad and the adjoining Silent Valley in search of "rare and medicinal species" to decorate their delicious dish. The tribes, unlike the non-trbes, are still loving nature and trying to protect the plants and animal life around them. They have understood the meaning and necessity of co-existence of plants and animals for the nurture of eco-system and for the existence of life on the earth.

SETTLEMENT PATTERN

Finding shelter or making shelter was one of the basic requirements of man during the course of cultural evolution, particularly when the prehistoric man moved from the stage of hunting gathering to settled agriculture. The tribal habitation assumes greater importance because of particular geography and specific adaptive strategies. The settlements of tribes, when compared to the settlements of non-tribes, are much more controlled and complicated due to their rural backwardness characterized by unique social systems and social orders influenced by ecosystem.

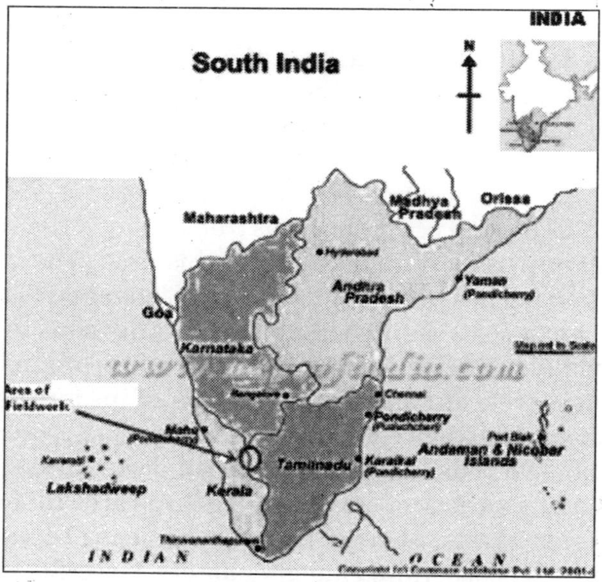

The Mullukurumba settlement is clustered, and is generally known as *kudi* or *veedu*. In Gudallur, the number of the Mullukurumba settlements is eleven, where there are 158 houses of both traditional and modern types. The number of Mullukurumba traditional houses in a settlement of Gudallur taluk varies from one to 35. In Wayanad, the minimum number of traditional houses in a settlement is four and there are more number of Mullukurumba settlements with more than 20 houses. However, the maximum number of traditional thatched houses in a settlement was less in Wayanad (24) compared to Gudallur (35) in 1990.

Figure 1: Traditional settlement

Figure 2: Guests are treated well

Pera has a unique appearance and is thatched with hay. Six bamboo poles support the roof. Materials used for roof construction are bamboo, reed, timber and other country woods.Walls are made of split bamboo plastered with mud and paddy husk. Every house has a ceiling called *pana,* which is made of bamboo splits, placed over a set of cross beams below the roof. *Attam*, a small structure of bamboo strips, hanging above the hearth from *pana*, is seen in all houses, and it is used for storing food articles. In almost all houses, a wooden box called *pathayam* is seen in one of the four corners of the single roomed house for storing grains.

Hearth, locally known as *aduppu*, is situated in one corner of the house on a platform called *chethana*. The particular stone used for building house is called *vennakkal,* and the soil used for polishing the hearth is known as *aduppumannu*. A small raised portion from the floor in touch with the hearth is known as *theepattam*, which is used for replacing ash simultaneously during excess burning, and also for placing the fuels in level with the hearth from the common floor of the house. Another raised platform, extended to the platform of the hearth, is known as *thannikundu*, which is used for keeping washed vessels and pots filled with water. *Thanni* in *thannikundu* literally means water and *kundu* means container or storing place.

Normally a house had only one room. The mud floor is usually plastered with cow dung and paddy husk. The Mullukurumba house has small *varandha, kolai,* round the

Figure 3: Waxing with cow-dung

house in its two or three sides. The *varandha* is constructed about three to four feet above the ground level. The houses with high *verandha* have mud platform of one-foot width running all around the house, one foot below the *varandha*. Some houses have two or three such layer of platforms, one above the other. There will be one or two small short steps to enter the house from the ground.

The wall of the house is painted with a solution of white clay. The lower portion of the wall of the *kolai* is painted with red mud, and the floor of the *kolai* and the sides of the platform are painted with a mixture of cow dung and charcoal. Drawing charcoal or chocolate lines with fingers decorated the wall.

The nature of houses varies from traditional and transitional to modern. The houses are classified into *kattapura, mudalappura* and *asharippura* in accordance with their appearance. *Kattapura* is the traditional house. As the term indicates, *kattapura* is made of a peculiar type of *katta* (unbaked mud brick) and is thatched with hay. *Mudalappura* is built with the help of bamboo. Baked bricks are not used for its construction. *Asharipura* is constructed by *ashari* (carpenter), and hence it is known by the name. The carpenter alone does all the work relating to the construction of the house. In addition to these houses, there is a peculiar sacred, single roomed hut called *valiyapura or daivapura*, which is located in the middle of each settlement.

MATERIAL CULTURE

In all communities, there exists a body of knowledge in fashioning implements, extracting or collecting materials and also for practicing manual arts and skills. This body of knowledge is known as technology. Technology is a system of knowledge rather than a means of production of material objects and artifacts. The knowledge of production and their use in the form of implements, weapons, and facilities is handed over from one generation to the other.

The Mullukurumba are agriculturists who also practice hunting and food gathering. For this, they use a variety of devices, and these devices can be classified into naturefacts and artifacts. Naturefact refers to natural tools and weapons, whereas artefact is an object modified or consciously manufactured by human beings for their use (Oswalt 1976).

One of the naturefacts used by the Mullukurumba is creeper. It is mainly used for tying things especially during the construction of houses. Tree twig is another naturefact, which is employed for catching crabs from the earth holes. Naturefacts like *kokka* (bamboo stick) is used for threshing paddy and the shell of *churakkai* (bottleguard) fruit is used as a vessel.

The Mullukurumba employ a variety of artifacts such as implements, weapons and facilities for the purpose of hunting, fishing, agriculture, collection of roots, tubers, non-wood forests produces, etc. Alhough the Mullukurumba are agriculturists, they still do hunting, atleast once a week. Hunting is usually a group activity. Individual hunting is conducted at times. The implements used by them for hunting includes: *villu and ambu, villu and mottu, kampivala, verry, kutty / pasha-kolu, narikuntham* etc.

Villu is a split bamboo about 3-4 feet in length. The bowstring or *njan* is of fibre of *manali*, a creeper, available in the forest. Whereas *ambu* (arrow) is a long thin shaft made of bamboo or reed, with a sharp pointed iron blade fixed at one end. It is used for hunting birds. When compared to *ambu, mottu* does not have a sharp end and is used for hunting rabbits and other wild fowls. Rabbits are also caught with the help of *kampivala,* which is a simple trap made of iron wires. V*erry* is a 'Y' shaped wooden implement with a piece of rubber fastened to the prongs. Small balls made of mud are used with this catapult to catch birds. *Kutty / pasha-kolu* is a bamboo stick, on top of which gum is pasted for catching birds. *Narikuntham* (tiger-spear) is a wooden pole with an iron spear at one end, used while hunting tigers.

Both men and women do fishing occasionally. The implements used by men are *kuthuvala* and *meenkudu*. *Kuthuvala* is net made of nylon threads and *meenkudu* is made of bamboo. Women catch fish with the help of bamboo net called *kortha* and the fish thus caught are kept in a bamboo basket called *meenkutta*.

Figure 4: Getting ready for fishing

Agricultural implements include *ngengal* (wooden plough), *nukam* wooden horizondal bar), *metty* (wooden bar to tie bullocks), *komma* (bamboo basket), *ancharp or cheruppu* (cylindrical long wooden block to level the field).

The household utensils of the Mullukurumba are very simple and are made of stone, pottery, brass, copper, iron, steel, aluminum, plastic, glass etc. They use different kinds of vessels such as *kalam* or *kudukka, chattikudukka, karichatty, kuttikudukka, palukachunna chatty* (all these are made of pottery), *cheppadam/chembu (*made of copper), *vattacheruva* and *panikudukka* (aluminum) for cooking. *Palukachunna chatty* is used only for boiling milk. Food items like *pittu, dosai* and *kuzhiyappam* are prepared in *pittu-kutti* made of bamboo or aluminium, *odu* (made of either iron or granite stone) and *karakundu* respectively. In order to fry fish, meat and vegetables, vessel made of pottery called *cheenachatty* is used. To decant or pour out water from boiled rice, an artifact called *chippilika* made of bamboo splits is used.

Food is served in bamboo plate called *manthalam* / *mannalam* or *choru-mannalam*. *Kolani* is also a bamboo plate and it is used for feeding dogs. *Karavala* is a bamboo stem used for collecting milk while milking cattle. *Kaylu, mukki* are ladles made of coconut shell. *Kutta and chada* are bamboo baskets for keeping rice. *Komma* is made of bamboo splits and smeared with cowdung for storing grains. *Chembu, cheppukudam* (brass), *tanny kudukka* (pottery) and *alumini* (aluminum) are used for storing water.

Panykallu, arakallu, kunthani and *mannukunthany* are used for powdering rice and other grains. *Panykallu* is made of two granite stones. One stone with a projected wooden piece at its centre is called *adikallu,* and the other stone with a hole in its centre is called *melekallu*. The projected wooden piece in the *adikallu* is thrust into the hole of *melekallu*. The grain to be powdered is poured into the hole of *melekallu*. A handle is attached to the end of *melekallu*. When this handle is rotated, the grains become powdered. *Arakallu* also has two parts such as a flat stone made of granite, and a rod shaped artefact called *kutty*. *Arakallu* is used to grind food materials. *Kunthani* (mortar) is a cylindrical block of wood with a central depression and grain is powdered with a long wooden cylindrical piece about five feet length called *thandu* (pestle). *Mannukunthany* is made infront of the hut with mud and husk.

Pullu-paya is a mat made of a special kind of grass, and it is used for sitting and sleeping. *Param* is also a cot made of bamboo; whereas, *parambu* is a broad and long mat like structure made of reed splits, used for drying grains. *Muram* (winnow) is used for winnowing rice). *Ury* is a sort of swing shelf made of creepers like *manaly, ketha* and *many*, and is used for keeping milk and curd. *Potha* and *mannuvilakku* are lamps. *Potha* is a bamboo stick with a cloth wound at the tip, and *mannuvilakku* is a small plate like structure made of mud. *Pichathy*, *arival, kacharakathy* and *vettukathy* are sickles/knives of different size and shape with iron blade and wooden handle and *atakka kathi* is a sort of knife for cutting arecanut into small pieces.

Thalakathi and *mudikathi* are knives used for cutting hair and shaving face.

Kodali (axe), *valiyuli* (big chisel), *cheriyuli* (small chisel), *ity-mutty* (hammer), *pullumanthy, pikkas*, *kaikottu* (spade) are implements used for chopping wood, digging earth, etc., and these implements have wooden handle with iron blade. *Parakolu* is an iron stick with a sharp end on one side. Mullukurumbas use two types of ladders called *eni* (ladder), which are used for plucking pepper. A ladder made of bamboo poles is also used. Cutting the side branches from the main trunk of the bamboo results in this type of ladder. Making holes at equal intervals in a long bamboo poles makes the second type of ladder. *Chatta, kutta* and *meenkudu* are bamboo baskets used for storing purpose. *Pelat* is a square box made of bamboo split used for keeping clothes.

DRESS PATTERN

Usually children below one or two years do not wear dress. The girls at the age of four years wear only a piece of cloth as upper garment known as *kettumundu*. It is wrapped on their body and by taking it below the right armpit; it is tied on the left shoulder. The right shoulder remains free. Boys started to wear piece of cloth around their waist called *thorthumundu*, usually when they reach the age of five or six.

The dress pattern of men is very simple. Men usually wear a white *mundu* (dothi) covering upto their knee called *velu-kambi*, and a white cloth over the shoulder called *panchi*. Men also used to wear shirts known as *pinnadan* shirts, brought by the *pinnattukar* (outsiders) from Karnataka State. *Panchi* and shirt are worn only when they go out. Usually, they purchase most of their clothes from *pinnattukar*, who visited their settlement occasionally. Mullukurumba male keep three items as an insignia, viz., *peesankathi* (a knife), *rool* (silver waist band) and *pakku* (a cloth bag). *Peesankathi* is always seen kept inserted in the *mundu* at the waist. *Pakku* is used for keeping betel leaves, arecanut and tobacco.

Traditionally, women wore a white *mundu* called *chuttukambi*, around the waist and it was tucked only at left side. This double folded cloth reached just below the knee. Another white cloth is used to cover the upper part and is known as *makkatti*. Like *kettumundu*, *makkatti* is wrapped around the body in a slanting position and the two ends of the cloth are tied on the left shoulder by taking it below the right armpit. The right shoulder is left uncovered. The lower portion of *makkatti* overlaps half of the *chuttukambi*.

Like dress, ornaments of Mullukurumba are also very simple. Most of their ornaments are comparatively cheaper and are made of copper, iron, brass, silver, plastic etc. Ornaments made of gold are rare.

Usually, black threads are tied around the wrist, ankle, neck and waist of a newborn. Children irrespective of sex upto five or six years wear common ornaments. They bore their ear with silver pin called *mullu*, and the ornament thus used after ear boring is called *bandumullu*. It is the pointed pin itself. It is bend like a ring and worn in the ear. Waistband of children is made of silver, and is known as *vellinool* or *aranjanam*. Bangles of children are known as *kaivala*. It is made of copper or silver or iron. The anklet is known as *kaavala*, which is usually a round ring of lead, iron or copper.

The traditional and symbolic ear ornament of unmarried male is *kathuminni* and that of married one is *kadukkan*. *Kathuminni* is an oval shaped gold ring having a square shaped disc in the front portion, whereas *kadukkan* is a small ellipse shaped ring of gold. Around the waist, male wears a silver thread called *thodare* or *arnajanam*. Men use copper

Figure 5: Kathuminni

Figure 6: Kadukkan

or iron finger rings only on the right hand fingers. Males do not wear any bangles or anklets

Figure 7: Kathumara

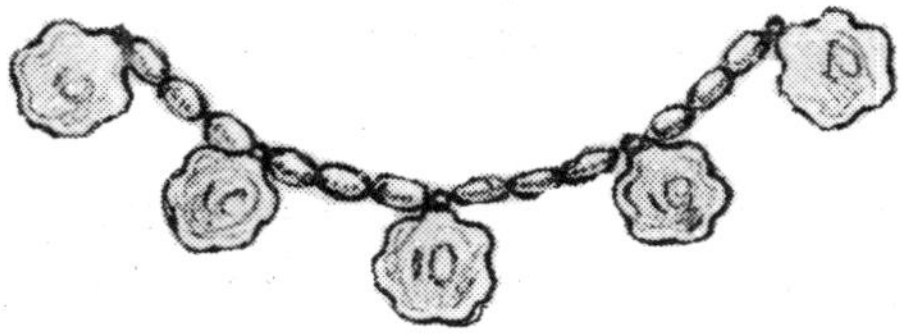

Figure 8: Kashumala

Usually, women wear more ornaments than men. The ear ornament of unmarried female is a round ring of gold called *kathumullu,* which is replaced by *manikathala* at the time of marriage. *Manikathala* is also known as *penkathala*. It consists of a round gold ring of many beads, and is worn at the top of the ear. *Kathumara* is another oval shaped gold ear-ring worn above the *manikathala.*

Women wear nose ornaments called *mukkuthi* or *mukkupotte,* only on one side of their nose. Females do not use neck ornaments made of gold before marriage. Their neck ornaments include *shangumala, panakella / kashumala* and *moorthathali. Shangumala,* consists of a number of round rings of conch, which are tied one another with a thread. *Panakella / kashumala* is a thread in which copper coins and plastic beads are arranged alternatively. Girls wear it after attaining puberty.

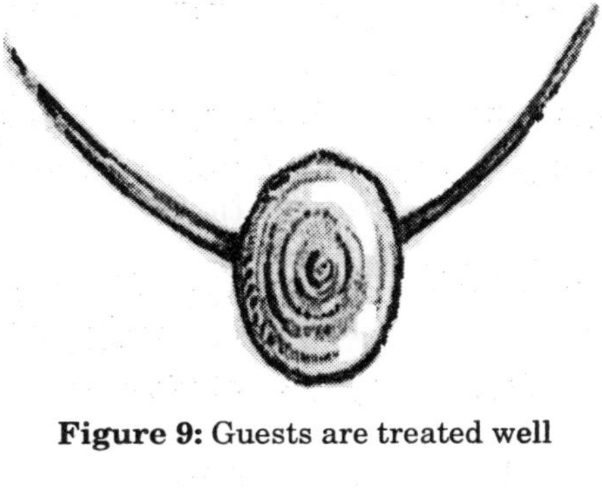

Figure 9: Guests are treated well

Moorthathali is a symbol of married woman. It consists of a single round shaped gold ornament known as *tali*, which is tied around the neck with a double folded black thread.

Females usually wear bangles made of glass or lead called *kaivala* in both hands. The bangles worn around the wrist is known as *pattavala*. It is a broad silver ring formed by the union of three to five narrow rings.

Figure 10: Pattavala

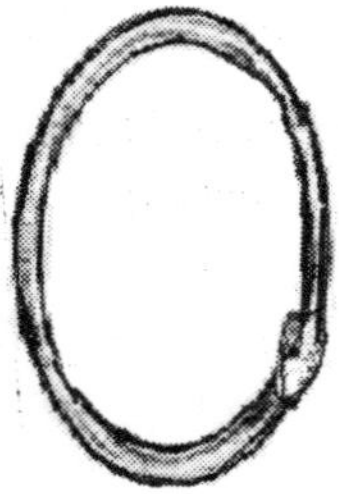

Figure 11: Tholanki

Tholanki and *chempadam* are bangles worn on the right hand. *Tholanki* is a single hard ring of silver, which is worn just above the elbow. *Chempadam* is a broad ring formed by the union of two silver rings. It is worn on the upper part of the right hand. Usually women do not wear waist ornaments and anklets.

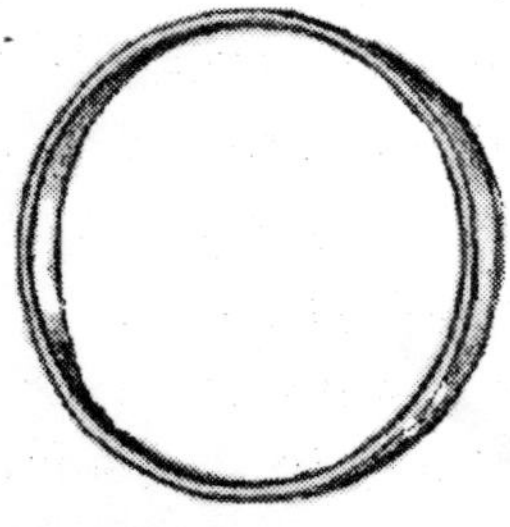

Figure 12: Chembadam

Both males and females do not wear ring on the index finger and thumb. Usually one, or two or three rings are worn in other fingers. Men used to tie their hair into a knot to the left side, and this traditional hairstyle is called *vattakuduma*. Women tie their hair and keep at the back.

Girls before attaining puberty usually fold their lengthy hair into several steps and tied at the backside. This is known as *madakkikettal*. After puberty all women tie their hair into a knot and keep at the back.

The Mullukurumba are fond of tattooing, which is locally known as *kurikuthuka*. Girls below twelve years old generally have it, and the tattooing marks on their hands and forearm are generally of stars and half-moons. Certain females called *pattukar*, belonging to the Scheduled Caste (Kurava), do tattooing. These women periodically visit Mullukurumba settlements and charge a nominal amount, depending on the design and labour involved in tattooing.

FOOD

Food is both biologically and culturally important as far as human beings are concerned. In order to perform various metabolic activities, biologically, food is inevitable for growth and survival. Different communities have different ideas, notions and concepts regarding food. Moreover, food pattern is moulded and shaped by culture and environment. The environment of Mullukurumba is rich with plant and animal species, and their subsistence pattern can be divided into direct and indirect subsistence. In the direct subsistence, materials that are gathered can be consumed directly and in the indirect subsistence, the materials are gathered and exchanged for money. It is further used for buying food materials.

The plant species that are consumed directly include roots, tubers, leaves, fruits, mushrooms, vegetables etc. Different types of roots and tubers available in the forest gathered by Mullukurumba include *nura*, *nara*, *korama* etc., and the availability of these items is seasonal. Some of the leaves consumed by them are *vazhacheera*, *chokannacheera*, *mutingachappu*, *kozhicheera*, *payarchappu*, *ponnamkanny* and *chembintal*. *Polanga, einichakka, echil, kara, ottamkaly, pana, talichi, athypalam, ummikkara, chullukai, nellachully, vetti, chalir, ngavalpalam, kotta, churi, nellikkai* etc., are some of the wild fruits collected from forest for consumption.

Mushroom is called *kuman,* and a variety of dishes are prepared with it. The types of *kuman* used are *katupotian, nedumtaly, perumkunan, ambukuman, naakuman, valakuman, pittukuman* and *vellasamkuman*. The Paniyan, another Scheduled Tribe living in the same area, also consume some of these mushrooms. Almost all mushroms are available in rainy season. Various bean varieties used by them are *avara, katankozhy, maravara, vilachy payar, pazhapayar, tattavara, tukayavara, neyyavara* etc.

The Mullukurumba also cultivate tubers like *kachil, chembu* including *karichembu* and *palchembu* (Colocasia sp.), *koorgal, pula* (tapioca), *nellakelangu* (sweet potato), *kulikelangu* (elephant yam), *chakkala kelangu* etc., and vegetables like *putymathan* (pumkin), *vazhakula* (plantain), *thakkaly* (tomato) and *velatanga* (bringal) in their own land for self-consumption. Grains like *muthary* (ragi) and *chama* (little millet) were their staple food, and earlier these grains were cultivated through slash and burn method.

The meat of rabbits, porcupine, wild goat, various kinds of pigs, black deer, dotted deer etc, supplements the food of the Mullukurumba. In the case of hunting, the man who killed the animal is given its head and one of the legs. It is considered as honour, and his family is supposed to prepare a curry with that portion and a share from this curry is given to every *pera* in the settlement. Almost all species of birds are caught and eaten. They are fond of fishes like, *kotally, mullan, totan, kongan, paral, aralu, katana, vala* etc. Two varieties of crabs viz., *karinendu* and *korothy* are eaten. The indirect subsistence of the Mullukurumba include pepper, coffee, turmeric, ginger, cardamom etc.

FOOD HABITS

Rice is the staple food of the Mullukurumba now, and earlier it was *ragi* and *muthari*. Food is consumed thrice a day. Like other societies, females usually do cooking. In the morning they prepare either *kathal* or *kanji* (rice gruel) and *chammanthy*. *Chammanthy* is prepared by grinding chilly, onion, *puly* (tamarind) and salt together on *arakallu*. Lunch is called *kenji* (rice gruel). *Kenji* is taken along with side dishes prepared with different vegetables, leaves or tubers. Rice prepared for supper is called *choru*. Mullukurumba are very particular that *choru* must be prepared fresh, and it is consumed hot. One side dish is prepared either with vegetables or with tubers. In addition to these, Mullukurumba prepare secondary food items like *nuralappam, panampittu, chakka pittu, kellupittu* etc.

Another important aspect of their food habit is that they do not have special menu for children, elderly or females; nor is any food item special for pregnant and lactating women.

Vegetables like *puty* and *mathan* are dried under sunlight two or three days and the vegetables thus dried can be preserved for months. Vegetables like *kaipakka* and *uruvilikka* are soaked in salt water before drying under sunlight. Keeping it on *attam* sometimes dries the food item such as *dosai. Dosai* can be stored for years by this manner. Dried *dosai* can be heated directly from the hearth and eaten. Drying in sunlight also preserves pepper, coffee, ginger, turmeric etc.

Meat and fish are preserved either drying under sunlight or by hanging in the roof of the *attam*. For drying meat, at first a *kol* (a tube like artefact) made of bamboo is taken. The meat to be dried is taken in this *kol* and is hung on the roof of the *attam.* The heat that comes out of the hearth makes the meat dry. This dried meat is covered with a cloth and is kept in a pot. They also prepare a sort of *chammanthi* called *irachypody* from dried meat. It is prepared by grinding dried meat with salt, chilly and onion.

Every culture has its own idea about food, and based on this notion, culture applies certain restrictions on the consumption of food. Such food restrictions can be seen among the Mullukurumba also. They do not eat beef. They also do not consume meat of monkey, *veruku* (civet), *utumbu* (Varamus bengalensis) and *keeri* (mongoose). In certain settlements, pigs that are kept in their own settlement are not eaten, but they are kept exclusively for sale. At the same time, they do not have objection to eat the fowls kept by them. *Kunykuny, kottakotta, tamarakuruvi* are certain birds, which are exempted from consumption. Likewise, mushrooms like *karatykuman, pillukuma, marakuman and angavalappan kuman* are also not eaten.

Usually, fish is not included in the feast prepared for festivals. Fish has a symbolic connection with death. On the third day, after the death of a person, one of his female relatives, along with other women of the settlement, is supposed to go for fishing. The curry prepared with the fish thus obtained is shared with others in the whole settlement. This may be the reason for not using fish during festive occasions.

Mullukurumba enjoy better health status when compared to other tribes like the Paniyan, Adiyan, Uralikuruman and the Kattunayakan. Mullukurumba believe that people of the older generation enjoyed comparatively better health status than the present generation. Earlier, ragi and millet were their main agricultural crops and staple food, and now these items are replaced by rice. They proudly used to say the local phrase *"Thalaum thakarayum thinna thadiyanu"*, which means that their body was mainly built by the habit of consuming leafy stalk and Cassiatora. They compare today's generation with the older generation by looking at their capacity to work and the ability to lift or carry heavy things. They say, "Today's three men are not enough to take a bundle of fire-wood carried by a single man of the older generation". This means that a single person in the older generation is worth three of this generation. They are of the view that in the past they used to work from dawn to dusk and rest only for taking food, but today people work little and rest more. According to the womenfolk, women in the older generation could make one *pothi* (local measurement equal to 52 sers) paddy to rice within an hour along with their duties at home and field. Another argument is that, in olden days, women used to pound 60 to 70 sers of paddy into rice, but at present, they are able to pound only 12 sers. Thus, it can be concluded that one who works hard and carry heavy things can be considered healthy as per the Mullukurumba's concept of health.

The Mullukurumba keep their *veedu* and *pera* always neat and clean. Regular bath is not compulsory among the

Mullukurumba, and they occasionally take bath during winter. Bathing and washing are done in ponds and streams. They use *cheenikka* (soap nut) powder or soap for cleaning their body. Oil applied includes coconut oil and castor oil (Ricinus communis). In order to rub the body, while bathing, they use fibres of *pinchika* (Luffaegiptica) and plastic threads. They clean their teeth either with *umikkari* (fired husk) or with paste.

The Mullukurumba mainly depend on well, *keni* (pond) and river water for their daily use. Well-water is used exclusively for drinking. They are of the opinion that water in the well gets polluted if used for bathing. They are also afraid of the fact that the well gets dried up if many people take water from the same well. Usually, women filter the drinking water with a piece of cloth before use. But they do not boil the drinking water. Their hamlets are devoid of latrines and are habituated to open-air defaecation.

Almost all grown-up males have the habit of smoking beedi and *churuttu* (rolled tobacco) and drinking of alcohol. Consumption of alcohol is compulsory for certain functions also. Irrespective of sex, they chew betel leaves, arecanut, and tobacco along with lime. Almost all adult carry these items in a special kind of bag, and they offer these to fellow men before chatting. Teenagers are also seen chewing betel, which they believe that it is good for their mouth and also for a pleasant smell.

Chapter - 3

ECONOMY

The economic activities of the Mullukurumba have undergone a series of changes from hunting and gathering to settled agriculture, and their priorities relating to economic pursuits have also been varied from time to time. In the past, hunting and food gathering were their primary economic activities and shifting cultivation was secondary. Later, shifting cultivation became primary, and hunting and food gathering had become secondary source of living. Still later, shifting cultivation was replaced by settled agriculture and hunting; food gathering and cattle rearing continued as a secondary source of income. What follow here is the traditional and modern economic activities of the Mullukurumba. A note on the land alienation is also given at the end.

The economic activities of the Mullukurumba include, hunting, fishing, food gathering, shifting cultivation, animal husbandry, settled agriculture etc. A clear cut sexual division of labour is noticed in their economic activities. Men usually do hunting and agricultural operations, whereas, women do gathering of various forest resources and minor agricultural activities along with their household chores. But, both males and females do fishing.

HUNTING

Nayattu is the local term used for hunting. According to Rajalakshmi Misra (1971: 57), the Mullukurumba hunting can be divided into four viz., *vili nayattu, valai nayattu, muyal nayattu* and *vilakku nyauattu. Vili* means 'to call' and etymologically *vili nayattu* is hunting by summoning the people. *Valai* in *valai nayattu* denotes trapping. Hunting of rabbit is called *muyal nayattu* and *vilakku nyauattu* (lighting of lamps) is conducted the day prior to the local temple festival known as *vilakku*. This hunting is done on the day of Vishu, in the name of the deity of the local temple, and the entire catch is offered to the temple authorities.

Hunting is a group activity by men belonging to the settlement. The forests lying near the settlement mainly are chosen for hunting. As a custom, they open the door of *valiyapura,* whenever go for hunting. Sometimes inter-settlement alliances are made for the purpose of hunting big games (See Annexure-1).

Specific forest areas viz., Meenmutti and Cherangode are assigned for big games.

Figure 1: Aiming for a kill

They also engage in another festive hunt known as *uchchala*. This type of hunting is not found among any other tribes of Kerala. All men and children, including babies start on a hunt; boys below fifteen and sick and old men are discouraged. The hunting group returns with the kill, which is ceremoniously cooked and eaten. The members perform dancing and singing till late into the night (Sasikumar 1999).

The Mullukurumba hunt animals like porcupine, rabbit, wild pig, wild goat, tiger, black deer, dotted deer etc. Dogs also accompany them to chase the prey while hunting. The man who first shoots the animal is given its head and a thigh apart from his share. One who catches or touches the animal first is given the neck and the intestine. The inner flesh (heart and lungs) is fried and eaten at the spot by all.

One of the popular hunting activities is *narikuthu* or *pulikuthu* (tiger catching). First of all they find out the rock hollow in which the animal lives. Then, a net made of fibre is fixed around the area in the forest where the tiger is found. Twelve or thirteen pieces of net are used for this purpose. One piece of net is seventy-five feet long and seven feet height. Thus, a large area of forest is covered by these net pieces. When the animal comes out of the rock hollow, it gets itself trapped in the net, somewhere in the forest. By making loud noises they search the area for tiger. Once the tiger is traced out, it is attacked with *narikuntham* (spear) from all sides until it gets killed. Mullukurumba also use *villu* (bow) and *ambu* (arrow) for killing animals. They also hunt crabs.

Mullukurumba eat the flesh of almost all kinds of birds except crows. They use bow and *mottambu* to hunt birds. Besides this, they also catch birds by using paste smeared sticks called *cole*. *Cole* is fixed on the branches of trees to give the appearance of dried twigs. If any bird, however big or strong, happens to sit on the *cole* or on the branch, and if its wings come in contact with the paste on the *cole*, becomes helpless to opens its wings and drops down (Rajalakshmi Misra 1971: 61).

FOOD GATHERING

Traditionally, the Mullukurumba were food gatherers of various kinds of edible roots, tubers, fruits, leaves, mushrooms etc. Certain items are available through out the year, but certain other items are seasonal (Annexure-2). Mullukurumba men occasionally go for honey collection. Honey is extracted for self-consumption. *Valyatenu* (Apis dorsata), *koltenu* (Apis indica), *puttutenu* (Apis megapis), and *kuzhuvatenu* (Mellipona) are the main varieties of honey collected by them. As the name indicates, *valyatenu* is big in size. *Valyatenu* and *koltenu* are found on trees. In order to collect them, two men climb on the tree, and bees are driven away from the hive by the method of smoking. Then the hive is cut with the help of a *pichathy* (knife) and comb is collected in a basket. Honey is extracted by squeezing the comb. *Puttutenu* is found in the hollows of earth and *kuzhuvatenu* is seen on tree hollows. Both are obtained by widening the hole with the help of *pichathy*. Honey extraction is done mainly in the Malayalam months of *Meenam* (March-April) and *Medam* (April-May).

BASKETRY

Some of the Mullukurumba are experts in basket making. The raw materials for basket making, such as bamboo, reed etc., are colleted from the nearby forests. The items like *meenkutta, kutta, kortha, chata, muram* etc., are made for own purpose, and the ordinary baskets are sold to outsiders. Now, only a few are engaged in basket making.

FIRE-WOOD COLLECTION

They also collect firewood from the forest for their personal use. Women and children moving with large bundles of wood on their head is a common scene.

SHIFTING CULTIVATION

In olden days, the Mullukurumba extensively practiced shifting cultivation as a primary economic activity. The major crops grown by them then were *ragi* and *chama*. They also cultivated a kind of paddy called *karuthan*. Before cultivation, the trees and shrubs of the area were cut down and burnt. *Ragi* was sown during the months of *Kumbam* / *Meeman* (February-April) and was harvested in *Chingam* (August-September). *Chama* and *karuthan* are also cultivated in the same land. After that, they leave the place in search of land for subsequent cultivation. The fallow period was usually about 4-6 years. Cow-dung and wild bushes were the only manure used.

AGRICULTURE

Agriculture is the main occupation of the Mullukurumba. Those who own land, cultivate in their own land and others work as agricultural labours in the land of outsiders. The lands that the Mullukurumba cultivate come under four categories viz., *vayal, thottam, uzhavu parambu* and *vettu parambu. Vayal* is the wetland used for paddy cultivation. The land almost adjacent to the *vayal,* but on a higher level is called *thottam.* Coffee, banana, jackfruit, pepper, arecanut, ginger, mango, turmeric, vegetables etc., are cultivated in this land. Both *uzhavu parambu* and *vettu parambu* are dry lands. In *uzhavu parambu,* cultivation is done after ploughing, but in *vettu parambu* cultivation is done by slash and burn method. *Ragi, Karuthan* and *samai* are grown on the *vettu parambu* lands. In addition to these items, tobacco, chilly and vegetables are cultivated in *uzhavu parambu* (Rajalakshmi Misra 1971: 66-67).

Major cultivation of the Mullukurumba includes paddy, coffee, pepper and tea. In accordance with the nature of cultivation, they divide crops into three, viz., seasonal crops, annual crops and permanent crops. Tapioca, ginger, turmeric, vegetables, plantain, chilly and sugarcane are the seasonal crops. Pepper is an annual crop. Paddy form both seasonal and annual crop. Tea, coffee and arecanut fall under the category of annual and permanent crops.

Paddy cultivation is the most important cultivation among the Mullukurumba. Cultivation is done twice a year and calls it as *nancha* and *puncha. Nancha* cultivation is done during the month of June/July, whereas *puncha* cultivation is in December/January. The main seeds used for *nancha* are *kothanda, kuttiveliyam, velumpala, thondi, palthondi, chamavazcha, jeerakasala, mannualian* etc. *Thaichinga, I.R.8, thaichoon, ompuncha, cherumoney, I.R. 20, mullanpuncha* etc., are the main *puncha* seeds.

The land is prepared for cultivation by *erupute* (ploughing) and by mixing with manures like cow-dung, leaves, potash and urea. Paddy seedlings are planted in this prepared field. Females mainly do harvesting. Bulls are used for *okkeluketttu* (process of separating grains from paddy straw). Paddy straw is either used for thatching their house or sold to outsiders.

It is said that Tarakar were the early inhabitants of the area. After them came Nairs, Nambiars and Chettis, a low caste Hindu. It was from these Chettis that the Mullukurumba learned the method of paddy cultivation in wet fields. During those times, there existed a practice called *koolamkuthal* in which the Chettis for converting paddy into to rice made use of the Mullukurumba. Through a long process of boiling, drying, husking and winnowing, rice was returned. The paddy was given in a measure called *pothi*. When one *pothi* (about 52 ser) of paddy was given for husking, the Mullukurumba had to return 20 ser rice. When 52 ser paddy was husked, usually about 24-26 ser rice was obtained. The Mullukurumba for their labour took the balance rice.

Arecanut seeds are planted and water it. The saplings arecanut are replanted in a new place after one year. Pit about one foot is dug and a mixture of soil and cowdung are added before planting the saplings. It starts yielding after seven years, and it is sold in market. They also preserve arecanut for their own use. *Adikola* is the high yielding arecanut.

Tapioca is cultivated during the month of September. First of all, land is prepared by making a series of pits and plant *poola thandu* (pieces of stem) in the pits. Yield is taken after 10 months. Tapioca forms the main food item for the breakfast.

Ginger cultivation is done after paddy harvest. Small *pathi* (pits) are made in the field and filled with ginger seed, *kalimannu* (brown soil), clay and leaves. Ginger is harvested after six months, and is sold in Erumadu ginger shop. For obtaining higher price, some people dry ginger and make *chukku*. Wayanadan ginger is the best type available in the State. Other types are *maran*, *ruiodi*, *vimala* etc.

Turmeric is cultivated like ginger in dry lands. Before selling, it is boiled in water, sliced and dried in sunlight. Turmeric seeds are preserved in *kalimannu* (brown soil) for the use in the next year.

Chilly is also an inter-crop cultivation usually done in the month of *Meenam* (March/April). Firstly a *thattu* (shade) is made to protect the field from cattle and fowls. Seeds are planted after watering the soil and later seedlings are transplanted on a well-prepared bed. Cowdung is used as manure.

Pepper is one of the major sources of income. The important types of pepper cultivated include *karimundi, chomala, balankotta, karimkotha, kattumoney, panniyoor-1* and *cherykudi*. Their soil is found fertile for pepper cultivation, hence no manure is used. *Murukku* is the main tree planted for pepper to climb on and grow. January is the harvesting season. Pepper thus collected is spread on the *muttam* (front yard) for a couple of days and are marketed in Erumade town.

In addition, they also cultivate many vegetables like *mathan* (cucumber), *chena* (yam), *chembu* (colocassia sp.) *karmosa* (papaya), *chakkarakizhangu* (sweet potato) etc., in wet and dry lands. Fruits like pineapple, orange etc., are also cultivated.

Tobacco cultivation is done on *uzhavu parambu* (dry lands). Tobacco seeds are strewn on the heap of cow-dung. When the seedlings have grown a height of two inches, they are removed from the heap and are planted again after levelling the heap. These seedlings are covered with leaves to avoid direct sunrays and are watered twice a day, about a fortnight (Rajalakshmi Misra 1971: 71).

Rajalakshmi Misra writes, "The tobacco plants are cut six months after the sowing of seeds. These plants are kept in the inner side of the roofs of their houses, for about two weeks to get dried. They are then spread on the open yards for a night so that the moisture softens the dried leaves. Early in the morning, the leaves are bundled and soaked in the water in which rice was washed. The bundle is then taken out and pressed to drain the water away and again dried. These leaves can now be consumed" (1971: 72).

Vazhakannu (plantain saplings) are planted during rainy season. Pits are made and cowdung and leaves are put in it. *Vazhakula* (bunch) is taken for self-consumption and also sold in the market.

Dry land is used for coffee cultivation. In olden days, the main item of coffee used was Arabi coffee, and now it is replaced by robust coffee. Harvesting season is January, and usually women and children are engaged in plucking coffee seeds. Coffee seeds are dried in sunlight for eight to nine days. Coffee dust is prepared mainly for own use and only surplus is sold. At present, they prefer tea to coffee as they get more income from the former.

Tea is an important cultivation as far as the Mullukurumba are concerned. Land is made ready by putting pits at an interval of six feet. After that seedlings are planted in these pits. The seedlings are watered with the help of small trenches near each plant. Manure and insecticides are also applied. The leaves are sold in the nearby Indico Tea Factory.

The inmigrants from southern Kerala introduced tea plantation in the area. ACCORD (Action for Community Co-Operation and Rehabilitation Development of the Tribes in Tamil Nadu) also helps them by providing tea seedlings, manure and other loan facilities on 100% subsidy. The Mullukurumba also enjoy the subsidies given by the Government. The details regarding the agricultural produces are given as Annexure-3.

Mullukurumba possess domestic animals like cows, goats, buffaloes, bulls, fowls and pigs. Cows and goats are mainly reared for milk. Young boys and girls, usually below 16 years or old men and women, who are no longer strong enough to attend heavy routine on lands, tend the cattle. Cattle is kept in *aala* (pen) on the field itself, *Aala* is a circular enclosure built with bamboo splits and its size depends in the stock of cattle one has (Rajalakshmi Misra 1971: 65). Bulls are mainly used for *okkelukeettu* (thrashing) and buffaloes are used for cultivation. It is said that the Mullukurumba learned the technique of buffalo rearing from the Todas, who lived on the hilltops of Nilagiri hills.

Usually, women are engaged in poultry rising. They leave their poultry free to have their feed during daytime and at night they are kept in a small shed on one side of the verandah of the house. Rajalakshmi Misra (1971: 63) pointed out that the eggs are seldom sold, but allowed to hatch because a chicken fetches a better price than an egg.

Eucalyptus Oil Extraction is the only small-scale industry found among the Mullukurumba. The main utensils used for this are *vattaduppu* (hearth), *chembu* (large brass vessel), *kuzal* (pipe), *veepa* (barrel) and *pullumanthi* (ladle). At first, eucalyptus branches are collected and brought to the *vattupura* (shed). Leaves are separated from the branches and are put in the *chembu*. Vessel is connected to the water filled barrel with an outlet pipe. Logs are used as a fuel and ladle is used to stir the leaves. The water in the barrel transforms the steam comes through the pipe into liquid and it is collected in a pot. Earlier, they gave much importance to the extraction of oil from *inchipullu*. (Zincona grass). When they found it unprofitable, they shifted to eucalyptus.

LAND ALIENATION

Land alienation is a universal problem as far as the tribal communities are concerned, and the Mullukuramba being a tribe is not an exception to this. The in-migrant settlers, mostly from Southern Kerala, are mainly responsible for the alienation of land among the Mullukurumba. The modus operandi of these settlers resulted in the transfer of acres of tribal land in the hands of non-tribes. The other agencies, apart from in-migrants involved in the land alienation, are the Forest and Revenue Departments of Tamil Nadu and Kerala, Govt. officials such as 'Adhikari' and 'Menon', Credit Societies, Banks, Heads of religious institutions etc. Lease, mortgage, registered sale, encroachment, gift etc., are the major forms of land alienation found among the Mullukurumbas.

Although there are a variety of reasons behind alienation of land among them, poverty is the basic reason for land alienation. Apart from this, their family system, debt, alcoholism, ignorance, expenses towards education of children, marriage and treatment of illnesses, expenses for buying buffaloes, seeds, agricultural implements etc., also caused alienation of their land. Like any other ethnic communities in the world, alienation of land has created unrest and tension among the Mullukurumba too.

Chapter - 4

SOCIETY

Social Organisation, in general, includes social institutions like family, marriage and kinship. The social organisation of the Mullukurumba revolves round the nuclear family, consisting of father, mother and unmarried children. Children learn the socially approved means of satisfying their needs from the family. In short, socialization process initially begins within the family. The term socialization means enculturation of persons and their assimilation into groups so that they can become active members of the society. Socialization and child development are inseparable. It is through socialization that people get their personalities moulded and acquire social status. It is the process through which human culture is transmitted from one generation to another. Thus, the socialization process begins at birth and continues unceasingly until the death of an individual. Important agencies of socialization are family, peer-group, school and community.

FAMILY

Nuclear family is the basic socio-economic unit among the Mullukurumba. Joint families are also seen, but extended families are rare. The father, who is usually the eldest male in a household, wields maximum authority. As mentioned earlier, there is a clear-cut division of labour within the family. Almost all household activities vest on the hands of females. Young ones are entrusted with elder siblings, when their parents go out for work.

As pointed out, the Mullukurumba children are brought up in nuclear families consisting of father, mother and siblings. The number of siblings and the nature of parents have profound influence on the child. Parents show much affection to their infants. Elder siblings also take care of them, fondle them and treat them tenderly. Both parents take care of them equally, as they believe that parents have equal responsibility in bringing up their children.

Childhood training practices may vary widely from one society to another. Among the Mullukurumba, the newborn is not given breast milk for the first three days, as they consider cholestrum as impure. Instead, during this period they give milk of any other mother in the settlement or give coconut water or grape juice. Cholestrum is collected in a cloth and buried. Generally breast-feeding starts on the fourth day and mother feeds the baby, whenever it seems to be hungry.

If a mother's milk is found insufficient for a child, they seek the help of a Chetti, *moopan* or elder members of the settlement. This chosen person gives a coconut to the mother after doing *manthricka* (chantings). It is believed that eating of this coconut helps the mother to lactate well enough to feed her infant. If it occurs that there is no milk even after seeking the help of a religious man, they start weaning on the15th day. The baby is given *kanji* (rice soup) on 15th day onwards. It is prepared in a small pot called *kuttikudukka* (mini pot).

Usually, infant sleeps with its mother near their hearth. This enables them to get sufficient warmth. Cradle is used only after three months. Bottle-feeding is rare among them; they use pearl oyster's shell, locally termed *kakkinnam*, or a glass or a spoon to give milk to the infant.

The Mullukurumba believe that the children who are well fed and well cared for are physically and mentally healthy, and the children who are neglected are physically and mentally handicapped. Therefore, they like to give nutritious food to their children, especially food rich in protein and iron, like fish, meat, eggs, greens to ensure them a healthy life; although they are not clear about what foods are nutritious or what foods contain iron, protein or vitamin.

Family, being a social unit, influences children in various aspects. In Mullukurumba society also the children begin to emulate their parents at an early age. By five or six years Mullukurumba children accompany their father, mother or elder siblings to the fields or woods. By seven or eight years, girls start grinding stone, sweeping house and perhaps washing clothes. By 11 or 12 years, they go alone to collect firewood. Both boys and girls care for their younger siblings. Girls, who assist the women after delivery, learn to handle infants and boys, who assist elders at the time of hunting, learn about hunting. Before puberty, both sexes would have acquired a reasonable ability in making a living and running a house.

Peer groups play an important role in the life of the child. It is the first social group, the child meets outside the family. It tends to condition his attitude towards social groups in general. It teaches the culture of the society and also the roles. Mullukurumba's attitude towards sexual matters is conservative. So the children acquire such knowledge from their peer-groups. Girls gain the knowledge of marriage, puberty, birth and other important prerequisites of life from peer groups. The elder girls of the settlement sleep in a particular house, and the elder boys in the settlement sleep in another house. Thus, peer-group is the most powerful and prominent agency of socialization in the life of Mullukurumba children.

Like family and peer-group, community also plays its own role in socialization. The community in which he lives conditions an individual's likes, dislikes, life's philosophies etc. One gets acquainted with various customs and ceremonies of his society through his participation in various activities of the community in which he belongs. For instance, *debar* is an initiation function, related to hunting. During this function, children are given trainining to use bow and arrow. The bow and arrow presented to children during this occasion is called *mottambu*. This function is initiated by *porunnavan* (headman of the settlement), who first shows a child how to use a bow and arrow. Then they go to forest for hunting. At night, there is a feast, and the meat of the animal hunted is an important item of this feast. During this occasion, elder members of the community tell their courageous and spirited stories to the youngsters. Thus, through these informal meetings and groupings, children learn more about hunting.

Another ceremonial function, on the third day after delivery, is called *bavali*. On this day, girls who have not attained puberty assist the newborn and the mother. During this time, they learn how to care and handle a child and also get knowledge on the duties of a Mullukurumba mother. It is also a part of socialization.

The Mullukurumba perform dances like *kolkali* and *vattakali* at the time of marriage and puberty. Children also participate in these dances along with elders. Thus, through these entertainments, they unconsciously acquaint themselves thoroughly with their culture. In addition, recreation also forms a part of socialization.

RECREATION

The Mullukurumba children show great interest in games. Their childhood is filled with games of diverse sorts. Boys and girls have different interests and budge with their own age groups. Children are made conscious of sex differences very early. Boys are encouraged to play together, and at games in which they initiate activities applicable to their sex. Both sexes make and play with toys and miniature household equipment. Boys engage in recreation as if hunting and fighting and may even imitate the dances they see and sing the songs they hear during ceremonies. So they become more aware of these sacred rites, at the same time learning their sacred songs, customs, rituals and ceremonies.

Boys are interested in plays, which need more physical work. Their important hobby is wandering in the forests. The environment also influences the type and form of recreation and leisure time activities of a culture. In the case of Mullukurumba children, they have plenty of space, lonely shaded woods and plenty of friends. On holidays, they go to the forest and collect firewood and catch small birds. During this time, boys actually learn more about their environment and they get informal education about their traditional occupation i.e., hunting and gathering. Each boy in a house has a *veri* (an implement which they use to catch small birds and squirrels). One of their important hobbies during leisure time is bird catching.

When compared to boys, the Mullukurumba girls are not interested in wandering in the forest or they are deprived of this happiness. They always stick to their house and its surroundings, and their entertainments are confined to this small space. Usually, they build small houses with tree twigs and pebbles and imitate their parents by preparing food. Plantain leaves are used as plates. In this play, elder ones play the role of parents and younger ones, children.

Plays can be divided into two viz., structured and unstructured. Structured games have laws and a pattern, and unstructured plays have no such laws and patterns. Structured plays among the Mullukurumba children are football, volleyball, kabadi etc. Unstructured plays are running, jumping, shouting etc. The school-going children learn new games from their friends. The elder ones are interested in football, volleyball etc. There are good players among the Mullukurumba who are members of the district sports team and represented many tournaments. Small children have many other plays, which have their own local names. A few of them are described below.

Thottu Kali (Touch & Run play) is one of the games, played by both boys and girls. A group of children are needed for this game. They form a circle, and one of them starts telling a rhyme, and at each word of the rhyme he/she touches a child, when all the children except one are left out they stop the rhyme. This isolated child is called the 'thief', who has to run and touch other children. It is continued until the child touches any one of them. While running they sing a song, which runs as follows:

"Aye, Bye, Suryan, Enne Thottal Papam"
Which means 'Hey, Sun, it is sin if you touch me.

Vala pottu kali (Bangle Piece game) is another game, usually played by girls. They collect different coloured bangle pieces in three or four numbers. One of the members shuffles these pieces and pass on four pieces to each member secretly. Then, each takes her turn to pass the pieces trying to pass out dissimilar colours and when ultimately one gets all pieces of the same colour, she becomes the winner and the game reaches to an end.

'Rubber seed play' is played by both sexes. At first they collect a fixed number of rubber seeds and scatter them. Then, they mark a line between two seeds, and hit one with the other. If one fails to hit the marked seed or hit any other seeds, except the marked one, he/she loses the game. They continue this play until one seed remains.

Chunkili punkili is an interesting game. Children form a circle, and one of them stays outside the circle and one stays inside the circle. The one who stays outside the circle sings:

"Chunkili punkili, kathaku thora, attinkuttiye konduva".

It means 'Chankili punkili, open the door, bring the lamb". With this, he tries to break and enter the circle. If the circle breaks, and he is able to enter the circle, he wins the play.

These are the common games played by the Mullukurumba children. These plays make them aware of the colours, vocabulary, measurements, rules, beliefs, etc. Through plays children learn how to behave in a group, and these also help them to build up leadership qualities and other skills. Thus, games also have their own position in socialization.

MARRIAGE

Marriage marks the most important transition from one social category to another, because atleast one of the spouses involved in it has to undergo a change in family, clan, residence or village. Like any other community, the institution of marriage among the Mullukurumba has its on rules, regulations and a chain of events.

The Mullukurumba generally follow monogamy, and instances of polygyny and polyandry are seldom. Marriages between consanguine, cross cousin and parallel cousin are not permitted. Likewise, levirate, sororate and child marriages are also not reported. Widows and divorcees are allowed to re-marry.

Marriage by negotiation is the accepted type of marriage among the Mullukurumba. In olden times there were instances of marriage by elopement and capture. The former is known as *odi koodal* (run and join) and the latter, *atru kadavu* (transporting from river side). In the case of *odi koodal*, the consent of the boy and girl was there and in *atru kadavu*, the boy usually kidnapped the girl from the pond or riverside when she was bathing or washing clothes. Another type of marriage is called *veetu kadavu*, in which father takes initiative in arranging the marriage of his son. Yet another form of marriage prevalent among the Mullukurumba, locally called *mukku vazhi* (three fourths of the way), in which the bride, who is always a widow or divorcee is met by the groom's party not in her house, but somewhere halfway between her house and the groom's house (Rajalakshmi Misra 1971:47).

Among the Mullukurumba, there are four *kulam* (clans) viz., *vadakkekulam, villippakulam, kathipakulam* and *vengadakulam*. Members of same clan cannot marry each other. Thus, tribal endogamy, clan exogamy and *veedu* exogamy are the marriage norms. Usually, they conduct marriage in the fifth months from *Kumbam* (February-March) to *Midhunam* (June-July). The reason for this may be that during these months their agricultural operations would have completed, and all of them are relatively prosperous. For them, Sunday, Wednesday and Thursday are the most preferable days for marriage.

The post-marital residence pattern among the Mullukurumba is patrilocal. But neolocal residences are also common. Usually, the house of the Mullukurumba possesses only a single room, which is used for both cooking and sleeping. Hence, marriage of a son makes it inconvenient for all. This practical reason prompts them to opt for neolocal residence pattern.

Traditionally, the question of inheritance of immovable property among the Mullukurumba did not arise, as there was no private ownership of land. The ornaments of a deceased woman/man are buried along with the body, while cattle, fowls, tools, vessels, cash etc., are distributed among the sons. Eldest son is given more priority in the inheritance of property. The matrilineal clans only have ritual significance and daughters have no right over their father's property. According to Rajalakshmi Misra (1971: 34), "...the Mullukurumbas are organised on one side into four matrilineal clans and on the other into several patrilineal lineages. The clan gains importance only in the ritual aspects of life. Whereas, in the inheritance of office and property, in the residence pattern and for authority, the society strictly takes into account the patrilineal lineages".

As the community allows remarriages of widows and widowers a year after the demise of their spouse, most of them get remarried. It is difficult to identify a widow from a married woman, as they do not suffer any social condemnation. Rajalakshmi Misra (1971:34) further states, "If a woman decides to marry after becoming a widow, she normally leaves her deceased husband's *veedu* on the evening of the pollution breaking day which is usually on the third or fifth day after the death of a person. Her parents or brothers come to take her away, especially if she is young and unable to decide by herself the course of action she should choose. But as long as she lives in the *veedu* of her deceased husband, no Mullukurumba from outside will ask her in marriage".

Mullukurumba looks upon marriage as an everlasting relationship and divorce is rare among them. Divorce is allowed on the following grounds such as if wife is barren; if either of the partners becoming unfaithful, irresponsible or fails to discharge their duties; if one of the spouses turning insane etc.

A man may divorce his wife on any reasonable ground, but he will not get back the *parisapanam* (bride price). But if a wife commits adultery and she is divorced, she should return the *parisapanam* to her husband. If the couple willing for a divorce on mutual agreement, the *parisapanam* is kept with the wife or her parents.

As far as the status of children of the divorced couple is concerned, they usually live with their mother, if their father does not come forward to make a claim. In all cases of divorce, both parties are free to remarry, and all the ceremonies are performed as in the case of the first marriage. The divorce cases are generally not taken to the tribal council, but settled between the head of the settlement and the elders of the concerned families. However, the practice of bride price and the return of the payment in the case of divorce act as a stabilizing factor in their marriage.

Joking relationship and avoidance are two kinds of kinship behaviour noticed among the tribal communities. Joking relationship refers to the custom whereby specific relatives may or must joke or tease each other whenever they meet. Joking relationship is commonly found between the affinal kins. On the other hand, the rules of avoidance, in its most extreme form, means that individuals, who stand in a particular relationship, as far as possible, ignore each other's existence and must refrain from social intercourse. They may not speak to each other, and if they meet on a path, one must stand aside or make a detour. Sometimes they may not even mention each other's name.

Among the Mullukurumba, there exist three kinds of joking relationship i.e., between a woman and her younger brothers-in-law; between a man and his younger sisters-in-law; and between grandparents and grand children. In all these cases, both parties make fun of each other without any prohibitions or restrictions.

The nature of avoidance is between elder brother and his younger brothers' wives, between father-in-law and his daughters-in-law and between grown-up males and grown-up females. It is noted that grown-up males and females taking care in keeping a socially respectable distance from each other. Usually, mother and daughters sleep together as one group and father and sons as another group. In the absence of two houses, girls go to sleep with their friends. Rajalakshmi Misra (1971: 39) says "People who keep avoidance relationship to each other are said to belong to *theendukulam* (untouchable clan) with respect to each other".

Different people in a society use different kinds of kinship terms in designating the kin of various types (see Annexure-4). Among the Mullukurumba also the kinship terms express certain obligations, privileges, rights etc., and these terms inherently depend upon the very superstructure of the society.

The Mullukurumba follow the classificatory mode of kinship terminology. The terminological classification in Mullukurumba kinship system is consistent with the behaviour of the relatives towards one another. For instance, Rajalakshmi Misra (1971:41-42) writes, "Father's brothers are given status and respect almost equal to that given to father. If one's father is not alive and yet one has to conduct a negotiation, either material or social or ritual, he has to take the guidance of father's brother. Thus, Mullukurumba addressing or referring to his father's brother as *peyappan* or *eyappan* (elder father or younger father) according to his being elder or younger to his father is quite consistent. Their wives are correspondingly called *peyamme* or *eyamme.* Similarly, mother's sisters are treated with respect as one would treat one's mother. One also receives all sorts of attention and privileges from their mother's sisters as they got from one's own mother and hence one calls one's mother's sisters as *peyamme* or *eyamme* meaning elder mother or younger mother, respectively according to their being elder and younger to one's mother and their husbands are called *peyappan* and *eayappan*".

It is also noted that the same kinship term is used in different sense also. For instance, the term, *ammayi* denotes both mother's brother's wife and mother-in-law. Similarly, *eyamma* stands for both mother's elder sister and father's younger brother's wife. Their kinship terms cover a large number of classificatory kins like *annan, aniyan, ettathi, aniyathi* etc. The children of the siblings of the opposite sex are cross cousins, and refer each other as brother and sister.

Rajalakshmi Misra reports "Use of classificatory terminology among the Mullukurumba does not mean that they hold all who are classified under one term with the same piety or emotional attachment. The piety or emotional attachment is normally maximum in the case of primary relationship, which gradually wanes and is less clear-cut as genealogical distance increases" (1971: 46).

POLITICAL ORGANISATION

The political organisation of the Mullukurumba comprises mainly of four regions called *nadu* viz., *packanadu, karanadu, neriyanadu* and *kellunadu*; and three hills known as *kunnu* such as *kottoorkunnu, kadoorkunnu*, and *edoorkunnu*. Below the *kunnu*, there are small hills and still below them there are settlements called *veedu*. Thus, *veedu* (settlement) is the smallest political and administrative unit of the Mullukurumba society.

Each *veedu* has a head called *porunnavan,* and his successor is called *porathavan*. In the absence of *porunnavan*, the *porathavan* presides over the functions. The succession of the office of the *porunnavan* is patrilineal and only the eldest male member is entitled to this office. At any point in time, the *porunnavan* of a *veedu* would be the eldest male member of that *veedu,* who is related to the previous *porunnavan* partilineally. As mentioned earlier, above the *veedu,* there are small hills and *kunnu*, controlled by *porunnavan* and *mooppan* respectively. The head of the *nadu* is also known as *mooppan*.

Of the four *nadu* mentioned, the *packanad* has eight *veedu* under its jurisdiction viz., *thirumakam, cheriyamma, illimbakam, kandaman* and *kurichiath, karanadu, neriyanadu* and *kellunadu*. The *mooppan* of the *packanad* is called *chellooppan*, whose position is reserved for the *porunnavan* of the *cheriyamma veedu*. The *Karanadu* is under the *nediyancheri mooppan*. There are eleven settlements under his jurisdiction such as *thachambakam, maattiyanbakam, ethirkunnu, olivayal, maandavakkara, monamkara, kollivatta, kenyambakam* etc. The *neriyanadu* comes under the *meppad mooppan* and the *kellunadu* by *kottachery mooppan*. In *neriyanadu*, there are ten *veedu* and in *kellunadu*, seven. Each *mooppan* of the *nadu* has a subordinate chieftain known as *nalappadi*, who is known with the prefix of his settlement. For instance, the *nalappadi* of *karanadu* is from *thachambakam* settlement and he is known as *Thachambakathu nalappadi*. In the absence of the *mooppan*, *nalappadi* performs all traditional functions attached to the office of *moopan*. They participate in life-cycle rituals like birth, death, marriage and initiation ceremonies. They also settle disputes in their respective areas either on their own or in consultation with the next superior.

The political chieftain of the Mullukurumba is called *thalachul* and his control extends over the entire Mullukurumba community in the Nilgiris and Wayanad. This superior position *thalachul* is held by the *porunnavan* of the *appadu veedu*, belonging to *Madoorkunnu*. The successor of the *appadu porunnavan* becomes next *appadu thalachul*.

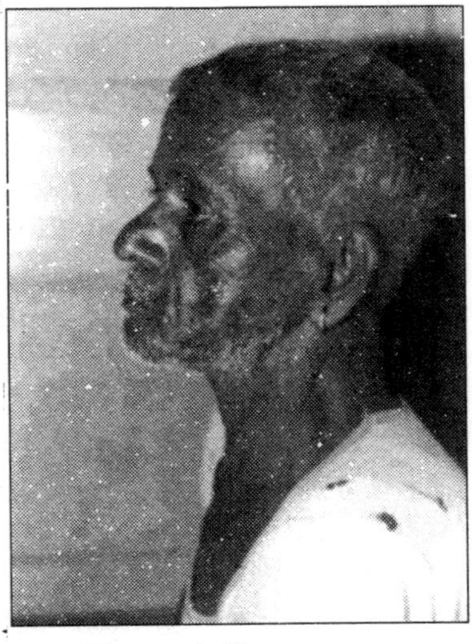

Figure 1: Porunnavan: recollecting the past

The *chellooppan* of Pakkanadu forms the intermediary between *appadu thalachul* and other *mooppan*. Passing communication given by *appadu thalachul*, keeping record of the proceedings of the annual council, writing decisions of *appadu thalachul* etc. are some of the major functions performed by *chellooppan*.

Porunnavan of each settlement places annual reports about their activities, disputes, measures taken etc., before the council. Important decisions are also taken with regard to the customs and traditions of the community. If any custom is to be changed, in view of the changes or development in the outside world, the decisions about it is taken in the annual council. Every matter discussed at the Tribal council is recorded by the *chellooppan*, and he also writes the order on behalf of *appadu thalachul* who endorses it by his signature.

Thus, we can see that there is a pyramidal structure of traditional Mullukurumba polity with *appadu thalachul* of the *madoorkunnu* at the apex and the *porunnavan* at the bottom.

However, outside this pyramidal structure, Kuppathod Nair, the leader of a Caste organisation, controls *appadu thalachul* who inturn has to seek prior permission from Kuppathod Nair for making changes. The supreme influence of this external caste leader can be seen in the appointment of *thalachul*. It is reported that, earlier, the *thalachul,* the supreme status, positin was given to *eruttumbon veedu*. But, once *eruttumbon thalachul* disrespected the authority of Kuppathod Nair by taking a decision of his own without consulting. A nephew of *thalachul* reported this matter to Kuppathod Nair, who took away the position of *thalachul* from the *eruttumbon thalachul* as a punishment, and it was bestowed on the nephew who exhibited his allegiance to the Nair by reporting the matter even at the prospect of inviting hostility from his uncle. This nephew who then became the new *thalachul* had shifted his residence to *appadu veedu* thus, transferring the title of *thalachul* from *eruttumbon veedu* to *appadu veedu*. Thus, the *appadu thalachul* has become the apex authority of the Mullukurumba.

RIGHTS AND DUTIES OF APPADU THALACHUL/ PORUNNAVAN/MOOPPAN

As mentioned earlier, *appadu thalachul/porunnavan/ mooppan* have to perform their primary duty as the *porunnavan* of their respective *veedu*. In the day-to-day administration, one of the major functions of *appadu thalachul porunnavan/mooppan* is the participation in life-cycle rituals like birth, initiation ceremony, marriage and death. They also play an active role in settling disputes in their area either on their own or in consultation with the next superior. Each ceremony relating to *veedu* begins at *valiyapura* in the presence of *porunnavan*. The *porunnavan* and his wife stay at the *valiyapura*, which is considered to be the abode of ancestral spirits, and it has got great religious significance.

In a birth ceremony, a newborn infant is brought into *valiyapura* and the wife of *porunnavan* performs the birth ceremony. This ceremony gives the infant a membership in the Mullukurumba community. If the infant is a boy, *porunnavan* has the right over him till his death and if it is a girl, *porunnavan* has authority over her till her marriage.

The initiation ceremony of a male Mullukurumba takes place on *uchar* day, the thirteenth day of Makaram, the Malayalam month. On that day, *porunnavan* gives bow and arrow to all male children who have to be initiated, which denote their change of status from childhood to adulthood. No Mullukurumba chieftains participate in puberty ceremony, as it is considered as a polluting ceremony.

Porunnavan plays a major role in the marriage ceremony. Before going in search of a bride for his son, a Mullukurumba male has to take consent from the *porunnavan* of his *veedu*. Then, he goes with a stick and sits in a corner of the *valiyapura* of the girl's *veedu* and distributes betel leaves to all those who come to him. He visits the girls' *veedu* four or five times till he gets consent from the *porunnavan* of the girl's *veedu*. On the betrothal day, the day for marriage is fixed and the boy's father gives four *panam* to the *porunnavan* of the girl's *veedu*. On the marriage day, the *porunnavan* performs a ritual called *daivamkanal* and finds out a suitable place for placing the *panthal.* The erecting of *panthal* on seven, six and four poles indicate the presence of *thalachul, mooppan* and *porunnavan* respectively.

Marriage ceremonies are followed by a communal feast, in which the chiefs are served first in the order of their superiority. When the couple visits the girl's *veedu* for the first time, they carry a bundle of dosa for the *porunnavan* of the girl's *veedu* who first offers it to the ancestral spirits and then distribute it to the members of the *veedu.* When the girl's family visits the boy's settlement, they also make a similar presentation to the *porunnavan* of the boy's *veedu,* who also makes offerings to their ancestral spirit and then distribute it in their settlement.

In the event of a death also, the *porunnavan* in the settlement is immediately informed. He gives permission to bring the corpse into the *valiyapura.* Then he throws a spade for digging the grave and an axe for cutting logs of wood for cremation. He pours water to the corpse first, followed by others. He leads the funeral procession to the cremation ground. On the third day, after the cremation, a purification ritual is performed under the stewardship of the *porunnavan.* He pours oil to the palm of the members of the *veedu* who apply it on their head and take bath. After bath, the *porunnavan* makes offerings to their ancestral spirits, which gives him a religious significance. In the communal feast that follows, *porunnavan* is served first. Thus, his inevitable presence at the social functions gives the office of the *porunnavan* a social significance

It has been mentioned that Kuppathodu Nair appoints the appadu thalachul. Since this Nair belongs to the Nellerote veedu, he is also known as Nellerote Nair. The Nellerote Nair is informed of the death of an *appadu thalachul* by the *porathavan* of *appadu veedu* who has the right to become the next *porunnavan* of *appadu veedu* and therefore, the next *thalachul.* Within thirteen days after the death of the *appadu thalachul,* the *porathavan* of *appadu veedu* goes with a bundle of betel leaves, 1/4 ser arecanut and 3.25 rupees to report the death. The Nellerote Nair accepts these offerings and elevates the *porathavan* to the *porunnavan* of the *appadu thalachul* and gives him a bunch of plantain and ten-ser paddy as offerings to God.

There is also a crowning ceremony, which is mainly a hunting ceremony, wherein all the invited chiefs should participate. The new *thalachul* should inform all subordinate chiefs about this ceremony. On a fixed day, before daybreak, the new *appadu thalachul* goes for hunting. He wears a *katcha* (cloth tied around his waist), bangles, and earrings and holds a knife with a silver handle. This apparel is the same as that of a bridegroom. Thus dressed up majestically, he goes to a particular spot and stands on one leg, holding the bow and arrow. *Chellooppan* who is the assistant, gives betel to all those who have gathered. After this betel ceremony, the *appadu thalachul* leads the hunt. A communal feast at the appadu veedu, in which ten youngsters of a particular veedu known as *pathu vallyakkar* (ten youngsters) prepare the items, follows this. These youngsters are entrsusted to prepare food for annual councils also. This communal feast is followed by their traditional festive dance called *kolkali* and *vattakali*.

Mattu (change of clothes) and *enna* (oil), stands for a purification ritual. Distributing *mattu* and *enna* is another major function of the *mooppan*. It is customary for a Mullukurumba to use the *mattu* supplied by a Vannan and oil supplied by a *porunnavan* to purify oneself and one's family after a period of pollution associated with birth, puberty and death ceremonies. The Vannan to supply this is traditionally identified. In the case of *Erumadu*, the *Cherangodu* Vannan has to supply *mattu* with ash contained in a bamboo. This ash is put in the water along with the clothes during the pollution period and are boiled and purified. The oil used for the bath is believed to purify them. A Mullukurumba, who fails to purify himself and his family after occasions that were considered polluting, are likely to be ostracised.

Traditionally, the *Erumadu mooppan* and other *mooppan* of the *kunnu* are obliged to supply *mattu* and *enna* to the *porunnavan* of each settlement under their respective *kunnu*. In return, the *mooppan* would receive ten-ser paddy and one ser rice for *mattu* from each settlement and twenty five paise per head for the oil supplied. Now, at the close of a birth, puberty or death ceremonies, the head of a household may go to the *porunnavan* of their respective *veedu* and obtain the *mattu*.

SETTLING OF DISPUTES

Resolution of disputes is a major area where the powers of the *porunnavan* are exhibited. Disputes are usually expected to be settled at the grass-root level of the *veedu* or settlement itself. *Porunnavan* calls a council of the heads of households in his *veedu* and discuss matters before Uchar day. If the matter is beyond his control, he refers it to the next higher authority ie., to the *mooppan* of the small *kunnu*. If a small *kunnu mooppan* has difficulty in resolving dispute, he consults the matter with the next superior. If *kunnu mooppan* or *nadu mooppan* could not find a solution, they report the matter to *appadu thalachul* for a final verdict.

The *appadu thalachul* settles the complaints that may come to him from these *kunnu* and *nadu* as an appellate authority. He exerts his powers and takes decisions when other *mooppans* fail to resolve disputes in an amicable manner. Such dispute settlement takes place in an annual council of the Mullukurumba to be held every year under the direction of the *appadu thalachul*. It is he who should preside over such annual councils.

When an annual council is decided upon, the *appadu thalachul* gives information about this through *chellooppan*, the *mooppan* of *pakkanadu*. The *chellooppan* passes the messge to the *mooppan* of the three *kunnu* and the four *nadu*. The *mooppan* of the *kunnu* in turn gives information to the *mooppan* of the smaller *kunnu* and the *mooppan* of the *nadu* to the *porunnavan* of the respective *veedu*. The *mooppan* of the smaller *kunnu* in turn passes on that information to the *porunnavan* of their *veedu* and the *porunnavan* to the members of their households. Thus, through their elaborate and systematic network of interaction and communication, the information from the top-most hierarchy reaches even the lower ranges and covers the entire Mullukurumba community.

PUNISHMENT

When a dispute from a settlement reaches before the *appadu thalachul* at the Annual Tribal Council, it is discussed and the parties concerned or their representative chiefs are given a chance to express their views in a very democratic manner, before finding out a solution. Usually, it is the majority decision that the *appadu thalachul* takes, although he formally pronounces the final judgment. Generally, the punishment would be small fines and the maximum punishment is the ostracism from the community. Ostracism is for major faults like marriage with members outside the community, non-performance of purificatory ritual, non-payment of fine imposed etc. Punishment ensures permanence and peace in the Mullukurumba community.

RELIGIOUS RITES AND FESTIVALS

The Mullukurumba are considered as ancestor worshippers. They believe that their ancestors had possessed supernatural power and protected them from all kinds of evil effects. Each *veedu* has a sacred centre called *valiyapura or daivapura* and all religious rites in a *veedu* are performed by the *porunnavan* of the respective *veedu.*

VALIYAPURA OR DAIVAPURA

It is a separate, sacred, single-roomed hut, in a settlement. In structure and construction, the *valiyapura* resembles other houses. It is decorated with black or dark–brown vertical stripes on the wall along with drawings and designs. All members in the settlement take the responsibility of thatching or maintaining the *valiyapura*. Men do not wear shirt when they enter *valiyapura* and women in traditional dress, i.e., *kettumundu*. Only white dresses are preferred, and footwears are not used inside. Women, during pollution period, strictly avoid entering into *valiyapura*.

The significance of *valiyapura* is that all rites and rituals connected with the life cycle such as birth, marriage and death are performed there. There is no special space for the priest among the Mullukurumba to conduct the rites in the *valiyapura*. The presence of *mooppan* (regional leader) or the *porunnavan* (leader of the particular settlement) is a must, when the rites are to commence, and the clan members of the concerned individuals initiate the rites. All people in the settlement consider *valiyapura* as sacred. *Porunnavan* has certain extra control over it, and he takes all decisions. For every ceremony, a part of the feast is cooked inside the *valiyapura*, and a portion of it is offered to their ancestors. Thus, they give prime importance to *valiyapura*.

Mullukurumba are not idol worshippers and do not keep any deities or photos inside *valiyapura*. Though the Mullukurumba do not keep any object of worship, each *veedu* possesses its own *kuladeivam* (clan gods). *Athiralan* is the principal god of Mullukurumba, to whom they offer prayers at the time of physical, social or economic difficulty. The other important *kuladeivam* are *Arivilli, Kalimala, Pakkatheyyam, Kandanpilli, Thampuratti, Poothalam Kallyari or Poothadideivam Gulikan, Vellakeliyappan, Thormathalachil, Kanyakarumakan, Vettakkorumakan, Vanadevi* etc. In addition, Mullukurumba also worship *Gulikan*.

Gulikan is considered as a god of disease responsible for the causation of good and bad effects. Worship of *gulikan* is prevalent only in Nedungode settlement, where a huge peepul tree represents the *gulikankavu*. They call it as *kolimaram* and women are not permitted to go near it. Breaking of coconut is the most important offering here, and it is done by the *porunnavan* of the settlement. In order to get back the lost possessions or belongings they offer one coconut and two-ser paddy to *gulikankavu*.

At the time of *uchar* (an initiation ceremony), a lamp made of bamboo called *kolthiri* is lit in the *gulikankavu*. For making *kolthiri*, a small bamboo stick is taken and its tip is split into three. Then a small piece of cloth is covered on the tip of the stick, and it is dipped in ghee before lighting. On *uchar* day, girls who haven't attained puberty, grind raw rice into powder, prepare *dosa* and offer to *gulikan*. These offerings are taken back and placed in front of the *valiyapura* for sometime. Then, *porunnavan* distributes these offerings to entire *veedu*. They believe that making such offerings help them to get protection from serious diseases or to obtain favours. Worship of *gulikan* has been observed since many years, and it is believed that it was started at the time of *thampurakkanmar* (kings). Besides *gulikankavu* and *valiyapura,* the Mullukurumba make offering to nearby temples.

ERUMAD EDAM ATHIRALAR TEMPLE

This temple is situated in Erumad village and is adjacent to the Kappala settlement. This temple has a role in conducting certain festivals of the Mullukurumba. As per the oral information obtained, this temple was built almost two centuries ago by a Nair Jenmi of this region and later, it was transferred to Chettis. A Brahmin priest visits this temple and performs *pooja* once a week and also during festival seasons.

The deity in the temple is called *Athiralanmar,* which is represented by a stone and a sword. But the worship is done in the name of Lord Rama and Lakshmana. They consider that when Rama, Lakshmana and Sita were leading a forest life, visited this place with the assistance of Uralikuruman, Mullukurumba, Chettis, Kattunayakan and Paniyan. In memory of these different tribal groups, they were given different roles in the temple during fairs and festivals. For instance, the Paniyan attached to the temple, called *pathrakkaran,* is supposed to arrange water, fuel and plantain leaves for the preparation of feast in the temple. His office is hereditary, which passes from father to son. It is told that at an occasion i.e., when the temple was under the control of the Nairs, the tribal communities like Uralikuruman and Paniyan were not allowed to enter inside the temple. Later, a *tantri* from Pattambi, Palghat district came here and after performing *prasnam* (divination), he had suggested the nature of offerings to be followed in this temple for maintaining its name and prosperity. Thus, these tribal communities got back their rights over the temple. In addition to this, the Mullukurumba have certain religious beliefs and practices of their own.

RELIGIOUS BELIEFS AND PRACTICES

The belief system of the Mullukurumba can be divided into three categories viz., supernatural, human and natural. Supernatural category mainly attribute to intrusion of evil spirit, wrath of god, breach of taboo etc. Sorcery comes under human category and natural agencies causing diseases are air, dust, smoke, heat, germs etc.

The Mullukurumba are afraid of evil spirits because they think that evil spirits are the ghosts of dead ancestors that can cause disease and misfortunes like fever, irritation all over the body, sleeplessness, self-murmuring, somnambulism etc. They feel that women and children are more susceptible to evil spirits. So in order to propitiate their ancestral spirits, they perform *ilakkukodukkal* (offerings rice, rice flour, *dosa*, chicken, mutton, toddy etc., arranged in plantain leaves) on the 14th day of the Malayalam month, *Karkidakam* (July-August). Mullukurumba believe that dead ancestors live in another world. For instance, in the case of a still born, soon after burial, the mother plants a sapling of latex secreting plant especially jack fruit tree and feeds this sapling with her breast milk for seven days, with a belief that the infant in another world would be receiving this milk.

There is a belief that some persons are born with evil powers in their eyes and falling of these eyes on other people, food, drink, cattle or any object will cause harm. It is considerd that when the evil eye falls on a person, the affected person feels feverish or shows abnormal behaviour or in some cases he may suffer with severe pain all over the body. In order to dispose of evil eye, elder one in the house takes a pinch of salt, chilly and mustard together, circumbulates around the affected person and put it in a burning hearth. If there is no smell, it is believed that the person is affected with evil eye. This is done only in night. Black threads or amulets are also worn in the neck or waist of children to get rid of evil eye.

There are many taboos in the Mullukurumba society. Clan exogamy is practiced among them and marriage within the clan is considered sinful. Adultery is yet another sin. They believe that breach of taboo of various kinds can cause diseases not only to the person concerned, but also to his whole family.

Koodothram (sorcery) is a voluntary matter and a technique, which can be learned by anyone for offence or defense. It is meant for causing evil effects on others. In the belief system of the Mullukurumba, sorcery affects only human beings and can cause paralysis, lose of speech and even insanity. Small plates of copper, bronze, silver, tender coconuts, bottles, fowl's head etc., are used for performing sorcery. As there is no sorcerer among the Mullukurumba, they bring specialists from Chetti and Kattunayakan communities. Specialists are paid money and arrack for their service. It is believed that an enemy can be killed or make him mad through sorcery.

The Mullukurumba believe that natural agencies like air, dust, smoke, heat, germs etc., are responsible for causing diseases like scabies, diarrhoea, dysentery etc. The Mullukurumba believe that diseases are caused due to wrath of god or goddesses, breach of taboo, sorcery etc., and in order to cure diseases, they wear *changola* (chain designed in a particular shape, made of a mixture of bronze, copper and silver), chanted threads, amulets etc. or perform certain religious practices such as *deviamkanal, kodiveykal* and *mudiyirakkal*. *Deviamkanal* is usually done by a religious practitioner called *velichapad* (oracle)

Velichapad (oracle) is the man who can communicate with the God or dead ancestor. A person when prepares himself for oracle, there is restriction on his food habits. He is not supposed to eat fish and meat. *Velichapad* makes offerings to the Gods on behalf of his clients. The performance of *velichapad* is called *vellatt*. A *velichapad's* assistance is generally sought when one is sick, and indigenous herbal medicines prove ineffective and also when there is an outbreak of diseases or when rains and crops fail.

Deviamkanal is considered as their important religious practice mainly used to expel the wrath of gods, as they believe that diseases are caused mainly due to wrath of God. According to them, the exact cause of disease and its remedies could be comprehended through *deviamkanal*. Sacred specialists like *velichapad* usually do it.

In Nilgiri district, there are no people who can act as *velichapad*. In Wayanad there are many specialists called *velichapad*. *Deviamkanal* is performed inside the *valiyapura*. The *velichapad* takes a bath before entering *valiyapura*. He wears only white dress, and a black *kacha* is twisted around his waist. While conducting *deviamkanal* the *velichapad* is possessed by gods like *vellakeliyappan* or *malampuliyan* or *kali*. These gods are identified by separate voices. *Vellakeliyappan* is identified by his howl and *kali* by her shouting. At this stage, as a mediator, he communicates with their gods through the method called *dharsanampidikal* and suggests appropriate remedies. Only men attend the *velichapad*. At the extreme stage of possession, *velichapad* runs inside and outside of the *valiyapura*. Throwing of rice by *velichapad* identifies that the whole programme is in the right path. Sometimes he propitiates some gods, folds a betel leaf with three pieces of arecanut and asks the indisposed to swallow it. This is believed to have a curative effect. After this, he becomes unconscious and falls down on *porunnavan*. Giving water to *velichapad* by *porunnavan* marks the end of *deviamkanal*. *Velichapad* is given money and arrack for his service.

Deviamkanal is also performed prior to marriage ceremony for knowing whether the proposal is good or bad and also to know whether this union will bring any harm to the couples. It is also conducted as a part of *uchar* in order to avoid the attack of wild animals and also to obtain a good hunt.

Kodiveykal (*Kodi* reading) is an art in which some Mullukurumba men have attained proficiency. This method is mainly used to find out the causes behind any disease or misfortune. The specialist, with the help of his tools (one sacred wooden plank and rice), finds the reason behind the illness and misfortune and also suggests the nature of the treatment to be taken.

If the patient is a small baby, he blows air from head to feet and chants prayers. If the patient is an elderly person, then while chanting prayers and burning camphor, knotted thread is tied around the neck of the patient. If the sickness continues, *kodi* reading is resorted. The *kodi* reader sits facing west, infront of a well-polished wooden plank on which he empties the handful of rice contained in a dried *koovala kai* (a nut) shell. Rice obtained by removing the husks over the paddy with fingers is used for this purpose. Invoking the god he makes designs on the heaped rice and takes out three to five pinches of rice. He then checks whether he had picked odd or even number of grains. Even number of grains predicts a smooth and automatic recovery from the sickness. Grains indicate the involvement of appeasing dissatisfied spirit of ancestor in the family of the sick person. The operation is repeated several times. A son, from his father, generally learns this art of kodi reading. Women are prohibited from performing *kodi* reading.

There is a legend behind this technique. It is believed that Paramasiva and Parvathi disguised as elephants. In order to find out the parents, their son Subramanian resorted to *kodiveykal*. From this, the tribe is said to have come to possess the technique of divining.

Mudiyirakkal (removing of hair) is usually done in front of a favourite deity in order to avoid diseases or to beget a child or to cure diseases. When a child is born, people may offer the infant's hair to their *valiyapura* for a specific number of years. This is always in odd numbers. The hair is allowed to grow, till this period is completed, and at the end of the period, the child is seated in *valiyapura* and the hair is cut by their family members. At that time, a small feast is arranged and people go to Pazhani, Subramaniya temple etc., for the same purpose. The underlying belief for this custom is that this ritual will protect the child from many diseases and misfortunes related to health.

Changola is a kind of chain designed in a particular shape and is constructed with the combination of three metals such as bronze, copper and silver. It consisted of 17 links (5 bronze, 3 copper and 9 silver links). An Uralikuruman or a blacksmith makes this chain. It is worn either on the wrist or on the leg in order to protect the child from death.

The wearing of *changola* depends upon the sex of the deceased person. If the deceased child is a male, the next male child alone should wear *changola* and if the deceased is a female, the next female child alone is compelled to wear the same. There is no room for worry even if the child born is the opposite sex of the deceased. The community follow this kind of practice from time immemorial with a belief that *changola* will protect their child from death. In addition to these practices, the Mullukurumba wear chanted threads, amulets etc. and also offer cash or kind to their own gods, *gulikan* and even other religious deities.

LIFE CYCLE RITES

Life cycle rituals play an important role in an individual's life. It is the transition rites celebrated to mark the passing of a person, or a group of persons, from one social status to another such as pregnancy, birth, puberty, marriage, death and so on. The life cycle of the Mullukurumba is marked by different phases and by various types of rites, restriction and prohibitions. Ceremonies are observed right from the birth of an individual to his/her death. The important among them are birth ceremonies including thread wearing, first rice feeding, naming, first hair cutting and ear boring, initiation, puberty, marriage, death & pollution breaking ceremony.

In every society childbirth is a happy occasion and it is true in the case of Mullukurumba too. They believe that children are valuable gifts of god and pregnancy is considered as a normal stage. Religious rites, taboos or restrictions are seldom observed during this period.

Normally, delivery takes place at husband's house. A separate room or extension of the main house called, *koochimuri* or *kusiniakam,* is arranged for the purpose and pregnant woman enters this room when labour pain starts. In olden times, women belonging to Paniya community provided their services as midwives. At present, the mother of the pregnant woman or any other old woman in the *veedu*, who attends the delivery, acts as midwife. Umbilical cord is cut with a knife called *muthari arrival* (ragi sickle - a small sickle used for cutting ragi), by mother-in-law or any other kindred woman. Placenta and umbilical cord are buried at a nearby place in the house. Turmeric paste is applied on the umbilical cord of the child and also on the body of the mother. It is used as an antiseptic paste. The juice of bitter gourd is applied to the mouth of the child. This makes the child to vomit the waste swallowed while in the womb. Both mother and new born are given oil bath every day by applying a paste prepared by mixing turmeric with wild tomato leaves.

Childbirth is declared by beating bow and arrow, if the child is a boy and if it is a girl, they beat utensils. This sound also declares a safe delivery and their happiness in welcoming a new member in their settlement. In order to protect the child from evil spirits, a small arrow (in the case of boy) or sickle (in the case of girl) is placed under the bed of mother and child. Though pollution relating to childbirth lasts for 15 days, they conduct a main pollution breaking ceremony, known as *bavali*, on the 3rd day after delivery.

This is the main ceremony associated with child birth. The newborn's mother's parents are invited for the ceremony and they come on the appointed day with a coconut and a piece of cloth. This coconut is used while preparing feast and the cloth is used for wrapping the infant when it is taken into the *valiyapura*.

On the day of *bavali,* a male member of the house, preferably the father of the infant goes to the house of a *Vannan* and brings *mattu*, after paying him a token amount. *Mattu* consists of ash, water and oil. Ash is taken in a piece of cloth, and it is tied on a bamboo stick. This ash is used for washing clothes used by the mother and the new born. Oil is applied on their body before bathing. Water brought from *Vannan* is considered capable of removing pollution. Thus, *mattu* is meant for purification.

The purification ceremony starts with the bath. There are two persons from their *veedu*, called *vellakaruthi* (lady) and *kuttikaruthi* (small girl) to assist the mother and the child respectively. At first they bath the child and transfer it to the hands of *kuttikaruthi.* Then the mother takes bath and wears a new cloth.

After taking bath, the mother and child enter into *valiyapura*. At this time, cow-dung is pasted in front of the *valiyapura* in a circle and a plantain leaf is laid on it. Child is kept on this plantain leaf for some time and before entering into the *valiyapura,* the child is covered with *mundu* brought from maternal side. Both the mother and child are seated in front of a *nilavilakku* (bell metal lamp) and are blessed with strewing rice and sprinkling water (brought from the house of *Vannan*) by the *porunnavan* of the *veedu.*

After this purification ritual, a feast is held. Main item of this feast is *pulikatchu* (soup prepared from sour mango), which is supplied to all children of the *veedu*. *Pulikatchu* is prepared from a wild species of mango tree. At first, the mango is ground well and its juice is extracted. Then, this juice is boiled to get its sauce and ingredients like coconut, turmeric and pepper are added to this sauce for making *pulikatchu.* It is an important item given to mother during pollution period. During this period, mother usually eats rice over-cooked with *pulikatchu* and *kurumulaku chammanthi* (well ground pepper salted to taste). During this period meat, fish and juicy food items are avoided. They also avoid as much water as possible in order to prevent bulging of belly. The feast on the day of *bavali* is prepared in *valiyapura*.

After feast, mother and child are allowed to enter their house. However, pollution lasts for 11 or 15 days. During this period, she is forbidden to touch household utensils or entering the kitchen. She remains in an isolated corner of the house.

On the 11th or 15th day when mother goes to bath, she takes all the things she used during the pollution period and washes them in river water. It includes bow and arrow/sickle, clothes, plates, oil carrier, bed, ragi-knife etc. The mat used on the day of delivery is burned at this time.

After taking bath, mother and infant enter the *valiyapura* and *muthi* (*porunnavan's* wife) gives *punnyaham* (water brought from the nearby temple by the father of infant), to drink. *Punnyaham* is sprinkled on the mother and child and also on all household utensils, symbolising purification. With this function the transitional period ends and the mother can resume a normal life known as *pettunannai*. Thread Wearing is done on the 28th day either by father or the mother of the infant and no ceremony is attached to it. First rice feeding usually takes place on the 6th month. This ceremony is performed at *valiyapura*, where the child is first fed by *muthi*, of the concerned *veedu*.

These three ceremonies are done together. The mother's brother of the child does usually naming at *valiyapura*, when the child is one and a half or two years old. He also does hair cutting and ear boring. No elaborate ritualistic performances are observed in connection with these.

Uchar, an annual hunting festival, is considered as an initiation ceremony. It is usually celebrated on 30th day of the Malayalam month, *Makaram* (January-February). Mullukurumba consider hunting as their traditional occupation and they think that their children too should learn hunting. So small boys are initiated to hunting on the day of *uchar,* which is an occasion for learning hunting.

Prior to this ceremony, *daivamkanal* is performed by *porunnavan* or *velichapad.* Then boys of all ages along with their father go for hunting. Older people also join them. While going for hunting, they take a special food called *pachappodi* (powder made by grinding beaten rice, coconut and jaggery together) in a small piece of cloth and tied around their waist. It is eaten while hunting.

Training in hunting starts with *panniyuruttal.* For this, bark of a tree is shaped in the form of a wheel. Then, it is rolled on the ground and children are asked to shoot arrows to it. The *porunnavan* initiates one child in this ceremony. This is followed by fathers initiating their own children. Only small arrows are given to the children. Real hunting starts after this ritual hunting. They are supposed to kill atleast one rabbit on this occasion and it is called *muyalkida*. After hunting, they take ceremonial bath and prepare a feast using the prey they hunt. A portion of it is offered to their ancestors and the remaining to all the members. Adventurous stories about hunting are narrated to their children by their parents in the night.

Among the Mullukurumba, when a girl attains puberty, she is secluded in a room called *koochimuri* by her sister-in-law or mother's sister. Only women and children are allowed to enter the *koochimuri.* She is visited by her relatives with *dosa*, *karakkund* etc., covered in plantain leaves. These food items are served to all those who visit her in her room. The girl, now called *manavatty*, has to stay five to seven days in

Figure 2: Offerings made at Valiyapura

koochimuri, and puberty ceremony is conducted usually on the seventh day.

On the seventh day, the girl is taken nearby pond by elder women and is given an oil bath with soapnut. Her dresses are washed with soap and ash. After bath the girl wears traditional dress, *kettumundu* and goes in front of *valiyapura*. She is given a special food prepared out of cooked rice, ghee and turmeric powder.

Figure 3: Preparing for a feast

On the same day at noon, men go for hunting and come back in the evening. The animal is skinned and meat is kept in the *valiyapura*. Rice is cooked outside and curries are prepared inside the *valiyapura* by women wearing traditional dress. *Kuttikurukka* is used for cooking rice to children. Two types of curries are prepared. One is with cucurbita and plantain and, another with pumpkin and meat. This is called *poothikkari*. A *nilavilakku* and a *thookkuvilakku* are lit, and then a feast is served to all. Men do serving.

After feast, men usually play *vattakkali* and *kolkkali* in front of *valiyapura*. Children are also taught to play these items. Special songs connected with Ramayana are sung during this occasion. Singing and playing last for the whole night and they depart after this celebration. It is significant to note here that *porunnavan* and other elderly men do not take part in these functions, as they consider this ceremony connected with pollution.

Marriage is conducted only after attaining puberty. They follow elaborate ceremonies in connection with marriage and are described here under the title pre-marriage procedure, marriage ceremony and post-marriage functions. One of the interesting aspects of the Mullukurumba marriage is that, the bride and groom do not see each other until the day of marriage. Usually, boy's father takes initiative for marriage. After informal enquiries about a suitable bride for his son, at first he consults the same with *porunnavan* of the *veedu* (settlement) and performs *deivamkanal* (god seeing) with the help of a *velichapad* (oracle). Then, he visits the house of the girl with a stick and a bundle of betel leaves. He is identified as *pennukaran* because of the stick in his hand. He sits on the varandha of the *valiyapura* and distributes betel leaves to all people in that settlement, and reveals the matter to the father of the girl and the *porunnavan* of the *veedu*. He is not given any reply on the first day. So he repeatedly visits the *veedu* four or five times with betel leaves and arecanuts.

Meantime, the bride's father consults with his relatives and friends and with their consent, he asks the boy's father to bring arrack or toddy for the next time. Thus, the boy's father along with his *moonnammuthan* (wife's brother) visits the *veedu*. On that day, they are received with hospitality and are given *paya* (mat) for sitting on the *kolai*. Boy's father offers liquor to the *porunnavan* and betel leaves and nuts to all gathered.

After these formalities, the *porunnavan* and the other relatives are invited for a formal gathering infront of the *valiyapura*, where the girl's father expresses his willingness to give his daughter and the boy's father expresses his willingness to accept the girl. Arrack brought by the boy's father is given to the girl's father. This function marks the sign for fixing the marriage and is called *pennukuri*. Date of marriage and rate of *parisapanam* or *kanapanam* (bride-price) are fixed on the same day. A week before marriage, both parties perform *deivamkanal*. *Parisapanam* is also given to the bride's family by the groom's father, a week before marriage.

Couple of days prior to the marriage is important as far as the Mullukurumbas are concerned. Close relatives come together a couple of days before the marriage and this day is called *banthuva*. The previous day of the marriage is called *alukoodal* and on this day distant relatives, friends and neighbours are invited. The marriage is conducted on the third day.

Usually, marriage functions take place at the *veedu* of the bride. In the morning, the groom's party goes to the bride's place. Before leaving, each one receives betel leaves from the maternal uncle of the groom. The groom's party is called *pennukar*. The groom's brother-in-law, called as *kanamketty*, carries *kanapanam* (usually Rupees 5 and 50 paise) and groom's sister, termed as *mundukarathi,* carries wedding dress for the bride; and these two are the important persons accompanying the groom. Besides them, two *thunakkaran* (guards) also go along with the groom.

After reaching the bride's *veedu*, the groom's party waits outside the *valiyapura* till the maternal uncle of the bride invites them into the *valiyapura*, where the marriage rituals take place. A *pandal* (a temporary shed erected for the purpose) is also constructed infront of the *valiyapura*.

At the time of marriage, a *nilavilakku* (copper lamp) is lit inside the *valiyapura*. Bride and groom's party stand on either side of the *nilavilakku* and the *kanamketty* hand over the *kanapanam* to the maternal uncle of the bride. Then, the *mundukarathi* and other women pull the bride to their side and give her the wedding dress.

Both bride and bridegroom wear traditional dress and ornaments. The groom wears a *mundu* and a cloth over his shoulder, called *melani*. He also wears a cloth around his waist, known as the *manavalan kacha,* which contains three colours such as red, white and green. *Kathala, manavalanvala, vellinool,* rings etc are the ornaments worn by the groom. The grooms' maternal uncle is obliged to supply these ornaments to him. *Kathala* is changed after marriage and *kadukkan* is worn instead.

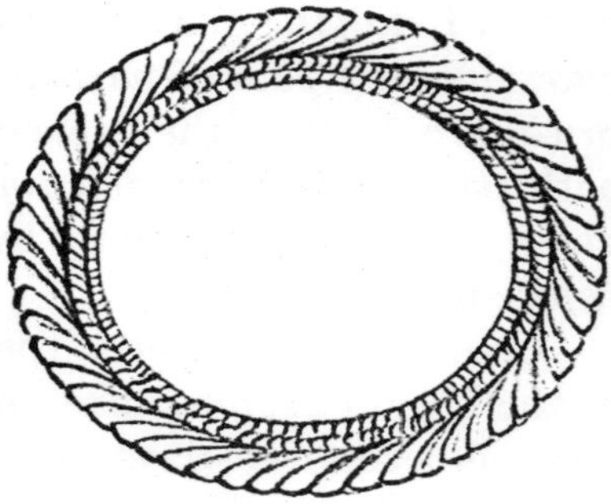

Figure 4: Kathala

The traditional dress of bride is called *kettumundu*. She wears this with the help of *mundukarathi*. The bride ties her hair in a particular style and this type of hairdressing is called *thalamurukkal*. *Kathala, manavattivala* or *pattavala, tholani,* rings etc., are the ornaments worn by the bride, usually given by her father.

Among the Mullukurumba, earlier, *tali* was supplied and tied by the maternal uncle of the bride, in the previous night of the marriage. The bridegroom himself ties at present tali. After this function, betel leaves and arecanut are supplied to all by the bride's party, followed by a communal feast.

Betel leaves are given to groom and bride by *kanamketty* and *mundukarathi* respectively. Bride and bridegroom take their feast in *valiyapura* along with other children.

After these functions, the bride is taken to bridegroom's house, fixing a date for *pittuvirunnu* (bundle of *dosai*) ceremony. When the party reaches the *veedu* of the groom, the mother of the groom takes the *manavatty* to the *valiyapura* and makes her to sit on a mat. All those who come to see the *manavatty*, put some coin on her lap, in return she gives them betel leaves. A communal feast is arranged at the groom's house at night. Feast is followed by *vattakali, kolkali* and *kaikottikali*. Men play *vattakali* and *kolkali;* and women play *kaikottikali*.

The very next day after marriage, the *muthy* (wife of the *porunnavan*), makes the *manavatty* to grind paddy and fetch water from *keni* (well), called *manavatti vellamkoral*. These customs formally denote that the new comer can accept the responsibilities of the female member of the settlement. Another custom is known as *manavatty meenkoral* (bride's fishing). Here, the *manavatty* is asked to go for fishing along with her sister-in-law. The fish thus obtained are distributed to all in the settlement.

Usually, three days after marriage, the couple visits the bride's house. A bundle of dosa called *pittu* is carried by the bride and distributed in her settlement. This function is called *pittuvirunnu*. The groom's relatives till the halfway accompany the couple. This custom is called *pathivazhi*. From there, the bride's relatives take the couple to her place. On reaching the bride's home, the bundle of *pittu* is taken to *valiyapura* and distributed to all.

During his first visit to the bride's house, the groom is obliged to go hunting along with some male members. The meat thus obtained is distributed to all. This custom is known as *manavalan nayattu* (groom's hunt). The couple returns to the groom's house usually on the 5th, 7th or 9th day. While returning, the ceremony of *pittuvirunnu* is repeated. The bride's relatives accompany the couple halfway. The *dosa* brought are distributed to all, and this custom is known as *marivirunnu*. *Pittuvirunnu, manavalan nayattu* and *manavatty meenkoral* have great ceremonial significance in the life of the Mullukurumba. It is supposed that after these formalities, couple can start a normal life.

Thus, marriage is a beginning of a new phase of life, and it is very important among the Mullukurumba. In olden days, both bridegroom and bride were not supposed to see each other until the marriage is performed. But now this custom has changed. The boy could see the girl at first and he informs his father. Then, his father and mother together visit the girl's house. They are treated with coffee and sweets there. Thus, marriage is an assimilation of a stranger into a group.

Among the Mullukurumba, when death occurs in a settlement, *porunnavan* is informed first, who sends messengers to relatives of the deceased, residing in other settlements. Then, *chavu* (corpse) is taken into *valiyapura.* It is laid on a mat and women are seated close to it. A lamp is lit near the head of *chavu.* Relatives of the deceased, who come to attend the funeral rites, such as, siblings, sister's children (adults), father's siblings, mother's siblings, and parents-in-law of married children are obligated to bring *kodimundu*, (a piece of new cloth, white in colour), betel leaves, arecanuts and tobacco. These are offered to the dead person. People of the *veedu,* where death has occurred, bring arecanut, betel leaves and jaggery. This jaggery added coffee is served to all those assembled, except mourners, who are forbidden to take any food or water on this day.

A short time after keeping the *chavu* inside the *valiyapura,* it is taken out for bathing. Two pieces of wood are used for laying the dead for bathing. By keeping the head on one piece of wood and rest of the body on another wooden piece, it is bathed in hot water mixed with turmeric powder. If the deceased is a female, her sister-in-law or her mother's brother's daughter is entrusted for bathing. In the case of a male, body is washed either by sister's son or sister's husband. Water is brought by *kulakkaran* (member in the clan of the deceased) and is poured on the corpse with the help of a coconut shell. At present, *porunnavan* pours some water on the corpse first. They do not take *chavu* inside the *valiyapura* after bathing.

Before taking *chavu* to their common graveyard, it is covered with *kodimundu* brought by relatives. If the dead person is a good hunter, a bow is kept in his left hand and an arrow on the right hand. If the graveyard is nearby their *veedu, chavu* is carried on a mat. If the burial ground is far away, a scaffold with bamboo is made for carrying *chavu.* Women are not allowed to go near graveyard.

Grave is made north-south direction with six feet length and four feet depth. The chief mourner (sister's son or eldest son) removes the first earth from the ground. At present, *porunnavan* initiates this and then by all other relatives. When grave is dug, a separate cavity is made on the northern side and head is pushed into it. This is done to avoid falling earth on the face of the corpse. Before keeping *chavu* inside the grave, it is taken around the grave thrice. If the deceased is a male, a small arrow is put in the grave. If it is a female, a small sickle is kept instead of arrow. Tools and dresses of the deceased are also deposited in that grave. Sometimes, ornaments are removed. Betel leaves, arecanut and tobacco are offered to the deceased. These are tied in a towel and put in the grave. 25 paise coin is also put into the mouth of the corpse. Then, they bury the dead and put three stones in the position of head, stomach and legs.

After burial, a date for *pulakuli* (pollution breaking ceremony) is declared and all of them return home after taking bath. When reached home, they clean their houses and *valiyapura* with cow-dung. They also cut down a plantain as a symbolic representation of the loss of a beloved member in their community. It is placed in front of the *valiyapura* and used for the preparation of a feast on the day of *pulakuli*.

Pollution related to death is observed for three to seven days and only vegetarian meals are taken by the mourners during this period. *Pulakuli* is conducted on the third day after the demise of a member.

Prior to *pulakuli*, they wash all utensils and sprinkle cow-dung water in and around their home. On the day of *pulakuli*, all men gather infront of the *valiyapura* and cut their hair. Then, they are supplied with oil from a vessel placed infront of the *valiyapura* for bathing by *porunnavan* of the concerned settlement. At present, oil is bought from shops.

Meanwhile women, from the *kulam* of the deceased, go for fishing, as they consider fish as one of the main items of feast. Feast is first served in plantain leaf and is placed inside the *valiyapura* as offerings to their ancestors. They close the door of *valiyapura* for sometime. Then, all gathered take food and depart with a decision to join for the next ritual called *kootathilkootuka* (confer membership in their ancestor's community). It is celebrated on the third day of *pulakuli*. This signifies the spirit of the newly deceased joining the spirits of their ancestors. Mullukurumba believe that if this ritual is not performed, the soul may wander without peace of mind.

On the day of *kootathilkootuka,* men go for hunting and women do fishing. They assemble in the evening and cook rice, fish and meat curry inside the *valiyapura*. Feast served in curcuma leaves are offered to their ancestors by keeping them inside the *valiyapura*. Door of the *valiyapura* is closed for sometime and when opened, children are allowed to eat these offerings. After this, all those, who assembled take feast and with this rites connected with death comes to an end.

FAIRS AND FESTIVALS

Festival is a social institution, which provides an occasion of gaiety for a group life. All festivals have religious sanction. The indispensable features of festivals are rituals and prayers followed by offerings. The festivals of the Mullukurumba include *onam, vishu, karkidakam-14* and *mandalapooja*. They also observe certain occasions like *puthari*, *parayedukkal* and *makarachovva*. It is seen that these festivals get into the society of Mullukurumba from the neighbouring Caste Hindus through the process of acculturation, and festivals distinct to Mullukurumba are seldom noticed.

Like neighbouring communities, Mullukurumba celebrate *Onam*. They make floral diagrams in front of the *valiyapura* for ten days and each day, before putting new flowers, the previous day's flowers are thrown on the roof of *valiyapura*. They take only vegetarian meals during these days.

The Mullukurumba call *Vishu* (the Malayalam New Year day) as *vishuvilakku*. *Kanikaanal* (the first auspicious view for the beginning of the new-year) is a special ceremony on this day. For this a bunch of Cassia flowers is tied infront of their houses as well as *valiyapura*. *Kani* is also prepared in the temple by a *poojari* (priest). It includes a golden bangle, a piece of silk, one ser raw rice, paddy, cucumber, coconut, small mangoes, small jackfruits etc. These are kept in a small shallow vessel of bell metal and are offered to god. People visit the temple early morning and give betel leaves, arecanut, musa fruits and rice as offerings. The Paniyan workers are given *mundu* (dhothi) and shirt. *Kaineetam* (coins given for an auspicious beginning and also for prosperity) is given to Children in the settlement.

During this time, they perform special plays in their temples. The very next day, in presence of the *porunnavan* the people of all settlements come together and conduct a special play called *uralikkali*, which is performed by the Uralikuruman. Karkkidakam 14 (July-August) is associated with ancestor worship where *baliyidal* (a ritual related to death) is done in all temples. For this rice, rice flour and flowers are offered to their ancestors along with *dosa*, chicken, mutton and toddy in plantain leaves, which is known as *ilakkukodukkal* (offerings made in plantain leaves).

In connection with Sabarimala pilgrimage *Mandalapooja* is performed by those who take vow to visit lord Aiyappan. They observe forty-one days fast from *Vrischikam* 1st (November-December) onwards. During this period, they take bath every day and consume only vegetarian food. Special offerings are made in the temple on the 41st day.

The word *puthari* etymologically means new rice. This is celebrated as a festival symbolizing the bringing of new rice into *veedu,* in the month of October. When paddy is ready for harvesting, they entrust a man belonging to the tribe Paniyan to cut a bunch of paddy. He does it after getting purified by a ceremonial bath. The bunch thus cut and brought is handed over to a priest in the temple for *pooja* (prayer). A portion of it is given to the Mullukurumba *veedu*. It is kept just infront of *valiyapura*, and the wife of the *porunnavan* is informed. She sprinkles water on it and distributes it to all houses in the *veedu,* along with the leaves of banyan or mango tree. These items are tied together and hanged up infront of their house and the *valiyapura*. Sometimes it is placed near wells, cattle sheds etc. It is tied infront of the temple too. A portion of the crop is offered to the god, in a *para* (solid measure), soon after the first harvest (December-January) season, and this ceremony is called *parayedukkal*. It is a symbolic expression of thanks giving for providing a good crop. The persons assigned to perform *parayedukkal* are a *poojari* (priest), a Chetti and a few Mullukurumba including a drum beater and a few others to play musical instruments. Before conducting the ceremony, front yard of the *valiyapura* is smeared with cowdung. *Parayedukkal* ceremony starts when *poojari* comes and sits infront of *valiyapura*. Two plantain leaves, one containing *para* and the other containing beaten rice, rice flour, raw rice, some flowers, sandal stick, Rupees 1.25, betel leaves, and one coconut are kept infront of him. At first the *porunnavan* fills the *para* with paddy and a bunch of coconut flowers are placed on the top of it. Then, the *poojari* does *pooja* and gives some paddy from the *para* to the *porunnavan,* who in turn puts it in their granaries. *Porunnavan* takes *para* and goes around the *valiyapura.* He then transfers paddy into a grain bag and takes it to the temple nearby.

The term *makarachovva* denotes two Malayalam words such as *Makaram* (a Malayalam month) and *Chovva* (Malayalam term for tuesday). As the term indicates, it is celebrated on the first Tuesday of *Makaram* (January-February) at the *Erassery Kali* temple, controlled by *Chettis*. On this day, the idol of *Kali* is washed in a nearby pond and taken back and kept inside the temple. At this time the *velichapad* (oracle) gets possessed by Kali and he goes in trance. Then, he takes a sword kept in the temple and dances around. After this, the Mullukurumba make offerings like musa fruits, eggs, rice flour, arrack, fowl etc.

Chapter - 5

SOCIAL CHANGES

This chapter examines various changes that have occurred in the way of life of the Mullukurumba, owing to culture contact, acculturation, urbanisation, intervention of various agencies, development programmes undertaken by both Government and Non-Governmental Oganisations, influence of Hinduism, Christianity etc., since independence. Major changes occurred in the areas such as settlement pattern, material culture, socio-economic relations, political organisation, beliefs and rituals, etc., are depicted here.

SETTLEMENT PATTERN

The *kudi* (settlements) of Mullukurumba had undergone vast changes within a span of two decades. In 1989, almost 92% of the *pera* were traditional (i.e., thatched) and only 8% were modern (tiled & RCC). A re-visit in the area of fieldwork in 2006 has revealed (see Figures: 1 & 2) a changed situation.

Distribution of Mullukurumba Settlements

Figure 1: in 1990

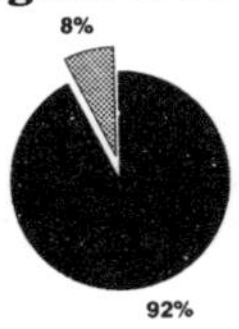

Figure 2: in 2006

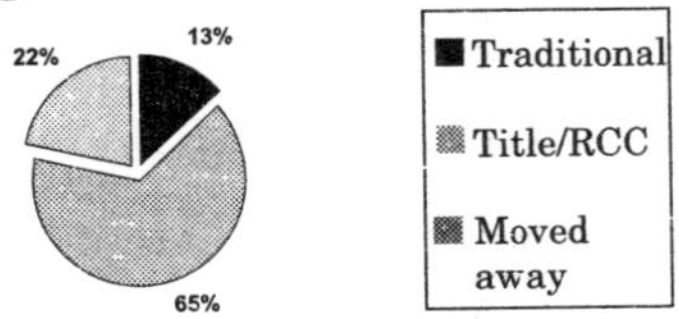

It is observed that 65% *pera* are modern (tiled or RCC) whereas the number of traditional *pera* is reduced to 13%. Moreover, cement-bricked walls and zinc sheets/tiled roofs have replaced clay-bricked walls and grass-thatched roofs respectively.

There are several reasons for the shift of house types from traditional grass thatched to tiled ones. One of the reasons is the scarcity of grass. This is because almost 90% of the Mullukurumba have adopted cash crop cultivation, instead of traditional paddy cultivation in both Gudalur and Wayanad. This has resulted in the paucity of grass even for their cattle. Another reason is that the houses provided by the Panchayath and other Welfare agencies were tiled or RCC. A tiled one replaces even the traditional grass-thatched *valiyapura* at Kappala. Moreover, educated and employed Mullukurumba prefer to build RCC or tiled houses with modern facilities. Thus, it is sure that the traditional grass-thatched *pera* will disappear from their traditional settlements soon.

Another aspect of change noted is that 35 families in Gudalur moved out of their *kudi* and built tiled houses in their own farm. The tendency of moving away from *kudi* and the reduction of the number of houses in *kudi* indicates the fact that, in the coming years, the clustered pattern of settlement will be broken down to nucleated ones resulting a series of changes in the traditional clustered colonies and group living.

The Adi Dravida and Tribal Welfare Departments in Tamil Nadu and the three tier Grama Panchayats in Kerala State through various development programmes have constructed houses, community halls, drainages, wells etc., in tribal settlements. Electricity and drinking water facilities are available in almost all settlements. Some of the settlements have been provided with solar lights.

MATERIAL CULTURE

A lot of changes have been noticed in the dress and ornaments of the Mullukurumba, mainly as a result of their contact with other communities. Men and women of younger generation prefer to wear modern dresses, while women of older generations still wear their traditional dress, *kettumundu*. Men now wear *mundu* and shirt. *Pinnadan* shirts are seldom used. At present, it is very difficult to identify a Mullukurumba from their dress pattern.

Marked changes are noted in their ornaments also. Their traditional ornaments like *pattavala, kaivala, chempadam, tholanki* etc., are disappearing from their culture. Now, only a few old women use them. Young females wear plastic, copper or gold-coated ornaments. Instead of their old forms of *malathali, kumbalathali* and *kunduthali*, they now wear only a single *thali*, which is tied to a golden chain. Pendant necklace and coin necklace are also not used by them now. In the case of men, they gave up the custom of wearing three to five pairs of *kadukkan* and tying *thodare* around their waist. Their traditional hairstyle, *vattakuduma*, has also disappeared and now, they visit nearby barbershops and get their hair cropped.

Changes have also been noticed in their utensils. Instead of traditional potteries, utensils made of aluminium, steel, plastic etc., are seen. Their traditional household articles made of bamboo such as *param* (cot), *pela* (square box), *karavala* (container) etc., are not in vogue now. In most houses, plastic chairs, wooden cots, benches etc., are seen. Books, pencils, pen etc., are seen in almost all houses.

Changes in the subsistence activities and the process of acculturation influenced their tools and techniques. They do not use traditional tools like *njenjil, panykallu, narikuntham* etc. Materials made of bamboo are also found to be very rare now. Thus, it may be noted that their tangible culture is on the way of transformation.

SOCIAL ORGANISATION

Family structure of the Mullukurumba has undergone very little change. In spite of the contact with the non-tribes, the structure and function of the family, have not shown any significant change from the traditional one. Nuclear families continue to dominate over other forms of families. Joint families are comparatively rare. They are well aware of family planning programmes and prefer to have only two or three children. They are also keen to give their children good education, nutritious food, medicines and all comforts in life.

Inheritance of property among the Mullukurumba is still through male line. Traditionally, the question of inheritance of property did not arise, as they were nomadic and practising shifting cultivation. They did not own land too. After switching over to the life of settled agriculturists, land became their property and such land is now passed on to sons at the event of the death of a father. When woman dies, her family members before burial take her ornaments. Compared to the past, women enjoy a good deal of freedom. They are frequently seen going out for shopping, marketing etc. However, a division of labour exists among them particularly on the basis of sex and age. Though post-marital residence pattern is still patrilocal, it is noticed that there is a tendency towards neolcal residence among the newly married couples living away from their main settlements. Avoidance relations practiced earlier have almost disappeared.

As could be expected, the economic organization has also undergone great amount of change due to adaptive capacity and close contact with outsiders. Added to this, the prohibition of commercial exploitation of forest, restriction in the practice of shifting cultivation, Land Reforms Act etc., have also brought about radical changes in their economic way of life. Their old economic system was primarily one of hunting and gathering. Shifting cultivation and cattle rearing were secondary sources of livelihood. Now, settled agriculture has become the primary source of economy of the Mullukurumba pushing down hunting, fishing and food gathering to a secondary source of living.

Earlier, a system of communal *pattayam* (property right) in the name of *porunnavan* existed in this community. In 1964, individual *pattayam* was given, which resulted in private ownership of property. It is followed by the encroachment of tribal land by outsiders, who took advantage of the simplicity and innocence of the tribal people, the Mullukurumba in particular. In short, the Mullukurumba were exploited by in-migrants for both material and other benefits. Thus, the Mullukurumba who lost their land were compelled to work in their own land as hired workers for low wages.

But for majority of the Mullukurumba, agriculture is the primary means of living. Though they cultivate banana, ginger, pepper, tapioca etc., tea plantation is given priority. This is because of the reason that tea plantation is more income generating and ACCORD in Gudallur and Tribal Welfare Departments in Kerala are giving loans and issuing seedlings for cultivation. Co-operative Societies in Nilgiri-Wayanad provide fertilizers to the tribes on subsidy. Most of their produces are sold in the nearby market.

The welfare programmes undertaken by various Government and Non-Governmental agencies, improved contact with outsiders, in both the states have influenced the Mullukurumba to diversify their traditional economies to modern economies where prime importance is for cash crops. A shift from their traditional economy to cash crops and wage earning has played a vital role in shaping the Mullukurumba way of life today. Changes in the socio-economic conditions and the degree of acculturation have brought about changes in their dietary habits and the pattern of expenditure. Further, the disappearance of tribal self-sufficiency due to culture contact has led to the decline of tribal reciprocal obligations. Money has great influence among them. Balanced reciprocity, which was prevalent among them in the sphere of tribal economy, has become a part of history.

However, the economy of the Mullukurumba is found apparently firm, if not stable, when compared to other tribes of the area. Moreover, many Mullukurumba men are employed in Government and other private companies. Some of them are even working in Banks, Schools and Railways. Thus, it is presumed that in the coming years, they might give up most of their regional agricultural practices and may become the part of the national or global economy.

Changes have also been noticed in the Mullukurumba political system. The traditional political scene was centered on the institution of *porunnavan*, *mooppan* and *thalachul*. But, this elaborate political structure is undergoing modification. Though *porunnavan* officiates as the head of their *veedu* or *ooru,* his importance is found to be decreasing day-by-day.

The modern Panchayath Councils and the Voluntary Organizations like the AMS and AKIMS in Nilgiris and the three-tier Panchayat systems and the involvement of political parties, particularly the LDF, in Kerala have changed the outlook of the Mullukurumba to a large extent. Most of them are now aware of the party politics, and youngsters took membership in political parties. In some houses, photos of political leaders and emblems of political parties are kept. They exercise franchise.

In short, it is observed that the Mullukurumba political system has now become a mixture of both traditional and contemporary forms. The first type is the product of their own culture in which political affairs are not functionally differentiated from social and religious matters, and the second type is the product of culture change due to culture contact with non-tribes living around them and interacting with them in their day-to-day life.

The changes in the religious institution are one of the factors that may happen, when cultures are disrupted by contact with dominant castes and communities. These changes are mainly due to the impact of Hinduism and Christianity. Traditionally, the Mullukurumba are ancestor worshippers, and each settlement has sacred hut called *valiyapura*, where ceremonies related to the settlement are conducted. There are no idols to represent their gods and goddesses. But at present most of the Mullukurumba worship Hindu gods like, Ayyappan, Siva, Bhadrakali etc., along with their ancestors, and visit Hindu pilgrim centers like Sabarimala, Parassinikadavu, Palani etc. Photographs of

Aiyappan and Goddess Saraswathi are kept in front of their houses. Ossimum plant is considered as sacred. They also observe a number of Hindu festivals.

The Mullukurumba are keen in observing 41-days fasting before visiting the Ayyappa temple at Sabarimala. During this period, they wear only black *mundu,* take bath in the early morning, eat only vegetarian food etc. These are due to the influence of Hinduism. The spread of Hinduism also makes the presence of Brahmin priests inevitable. Thus, the authority of the traditional political leader, and the dignity of the office of the *porunnavan* are fading away. His role in the day-to-day religious rituals is becoming immaterial.

In the past, when they fell ill, they worshipped their ancestors. But at present, offerings are made in temples, in addition to *poojas*. Offerings are also made to nearby churches, whenever they suffer from incurable diseases. They also visit hospitals and seek medical advice.

In addition to these, culture contact has resulted significant changes in the ritual ceremonies connected with birth and marriage. The ceremonies associated with childbirth are gradually disappearing from the Mullukurumba society. There are many reasons for this. The younger generation prefers hospitalization at the time of delivery. In such cases, they bring *punniyaham* (holy water) from the nearby temple and sprinkle it on the mother and child. Due to the contact with non-tribes, they have adopted many of the practices of the non-tribes and ignored their own customs. Now, they started recording the date of birth and birth star of newborns.

In olden times, ceremonies connected with naming, first hair cutting, ear boring and first rice feeding were done in *valiyapura.* At present, these are done in temples. The parents select name and father calls the name three times. This is done, when the child is one and-a-half or two years old. It is noticed that many of them have adopted popular Caste Hindu names instead of their usual names indicating tribal identity and status.

As mentioned earlier, first hair cutting was also done in temples as an offering, if the child was affected with any incurable disease. In olden times, both males and females used to bore their ears. But at present, it is done only for girls. An uncle with a silver pin usually does it. If it is done at a temple, the priest does it. For first rice feeding of a child, Parassini Madappura Muthappan, Guruvayoor Sree Krishna temple etc., are visited.

Marked changes could be noted in the Mullukurumba marriage. The traditional practice of performing actual marriage rites at the *valiyapura* is disappearing. The educated and economically well off Mullukurumba prefer to perform marriage ceremonies in the temple.

Not only is the venue of marriage, but traditional marriage dress and ornaments are also undergoing changes. Distribution of wedding cards, participation of outsiders, presence of *panthal,* influence of modern technical instruments etc., are typical examples highlighting changes in the Mullukurumba marriage system. The role of matri-kin in marriage ceremony is now minimized. The groom himself, instead of the bride's *ammavan*, ties *thali.* Moreover, the role of the *porunnavan* is also being decreased or replaced by a temple priest. All these changes are attributed to the influence of Caste Hindus, who form the reference group of the Mullukurumba.

Various welfare programmes undertaken by both the Government and NGOs (see Annexure 5–A & B) made remarkable changes in the life-style of the Mullukurumba, especially in the realm of housing, occupation, education, health and communication. Changes noticed in housing and occupations are already described above. Hence, this section is confined to the rest of the areas such as education, health and communication.

Education is a major factor in improving the social status, and enables the members of a society to play new roles in the changing situation. As far as the Mullukurumba are concerned, the present generation gives tremendous importance to education as a means of achieving upward social mobility. The GTRS started at Kappala in 1968, as an Upper Primary School, has now become a Higher Secondary School with a stadium in its credit. The Adult Education Programme of the Government and ACCORD in Gudallur has also helped the Mullukurumba to reach their literacy at a higher level.

Moreover, the educated Mullukurumba could interact with other tribes and non-tribes freely. They also keep pace with the outside world by reading newspapers, journals, going to movies etc. Their standard of living too has changed. Education has contributed a great deal in their transformation.

Like any other tribes, the religious practices of Mullukurumba too are directly or indirectly associated with their health concepts. Earlier, they believed that diseases are caused due to wrath of god or goddesses, breach of taboo, sorcery etc., and sought the help of religious practitioners to perform religious practices such as *deviamkanal, kodiveykal* and *mudiyirakkal*, for curing illness. But, now, the situation has changed owing to their contact with other cultures.

Mullukurumba is a fast changing society adjusting with the changing world. Now, they visit hospitals and seek medical advice. Midwives and doctors regularly visit their settlements and give instructions to the needy. Doctors appointed in Public Health Centers visit the settlements regularly and give them treatment and medicines.

Other factors that affect the health condition of the people directly or indirectly are land-alienation, deforestation and forest policy. Forest had provided resources for a comfortable life. Deforestation has resulted in the disappearance of valuable and precious medicinal plants, roots, tubers fruits etc. Timber, rosewood, country-wood, eucalyptus, bamboo etc., became rare. Mullukurumba was traditionally a hunting and gathering tribe and earned much of their food by hunting, fishing and collecting roots and tubers. This has become a sweet memory of the past, since the implementation of new forest policy and deforestation.

Two or three examples are sufficient to show the impact of deforestation and new forest policy upon their health. In olden days, enormous *mananthakkali* (a kind of fruit, contains vitamin B) was available in the forest, which was a favourite item for their children. But, deforestation resulted in the extinction of this plant and its non-consumption caused vitamin B deficiency, especially among the children.

When forests vanished, animals and birds and rare species of honeybees also disappeared. Traditionally, these people used to hunt animals and birds, which was the main source of protein. This gave them the major share of their energy and enabled them to resist many diseases. Now, the occasional hunts give them either a rabbit or a porcupine. The most unfortunate thing is that still they did not make any attempt to compensate their loss.

Most of the valuable trees and rare medicinal plants have been ruined by the in-migrants for the cultivation of commercial crops and establishing residential palaces and townships. Many traditional practitioners complained about scarcity of useful plants. Fishing has stopped almost completely. The shift from ragi, millet etc., to rice has also considerably lessened the nutritional content of their diet.

COMMUNICATION

According to Rajalakshmi Misra (1971: 3), "there was only one cart tract running through this village which has been converted into a metalled road about nine years ago. Bus now ply on this road twice a day between Gudalur and Chulliyode, the latter leading to Sultan Battery" This was the situation of Erumad village almost a half-century ago.

Now, the situation has changed and transportation facilities have increased manifold than in 1960s and 90s. Almost all colonies have Panchayath roads and sub-roads. It is noticed that settlements like Kappala, Theyyakkuni and Onimoola are connected through a Panchayath road, constructed by the Cherambadi Panchayath. Frequent and regular services of both KSRTC and private buses from Sulthan Bathery to Cherambadi and Gudallur via Kappala have resulted in frequent contact with a number of townships spread over in Gudalur and Wayanad. Availability of jeeps and autorickshaws makes road communication possible even at late nights. Moreover, Erumadu, which is situated at the center of all these settlements, has now become a full-fledged rural township with Internet café and BSNL tower. Many Mullukurumba possess cell phones. Another area where change noticed is the mass media. Many Mullukurumba now read newspapers and many of them have Televisions and land Telephones.

INTERACTION WITH OTHER COMMUNITIES

The Mullukurumba have frequent contact with different castes and tribes of the areas. On various economic, social and religious occasions, the Mullukurumba interact with different tribes and castes, according to their tradition. The interaction affected their culture and brought about change in it.

During 1960s, in addition to Mullukurumba, various communities like Chetty, Urali Kuruman, Kattunayakan, Paniyan, Adiyan etc., inhabited Gudalur and Wayanad. Among these communities, Chetty enjoyed highest social

Figure 3: Inter-tribal interaction

status locally, followed by the Mullukurumba. In social status, Uralikuruman, Kattunayakan and Paniyan stand below the Mullukurumba. Thus, it is seen that Mullukurumba were just below only to Chetty in social and ritual status but lead the other three tribes viz., Urali Kuruman, Kattunayakan, Paniyan. Rajalakshmi Misra (1971:31) observes:

> "In the economic sphere some Mullukurumbas work on the fields of Chettys for wages. Kattu Naickens work on the fields of Mullukurumbas and Chettys, for daily wages. The Mullukurumbas and Chettys pay in kind or cash to the Urali Kurumbas who meet their demands of iron implements, pottery wares, baskets, etc., in which the latter are proficient. The Paniyans, who are tied to the lands owned by the Chettys, owe certain obligations to Mullukurumbas on ceremonial occasions. They are paid in kind by the latter. Thus, there are social, economic and ritual ties amongst the natives of Erumad, though each group may live in separate uniethnic settlements".

The Mullukurumba maintained economic interaction with the in-migrant Muslims and Christians. However, their contact with communities like Brahmins and Nairs was minimum. The Figure 4 given below shows the pattern of social interaction between the Mullukurumba and the neighbouring communities during 1960s.

In this figure, the dark and broad outer circle shows the interaction among the different communities listed. The narrow circles with arrow marks inside the broad circle point out the interaction between two groups. The inner pointed lines indicate the nature of interaction between Mullukurumba and other communities.

It is observed that the interactions between Mullukurumba and other communities have increased manifold during 1980s and '90s and now they have permanent association with Chetty, Christian and Muslim immigrants. The nature of interaction between the Mullukurumba and the neighbouring communities during 1990s is portrayed in the Figure 5.

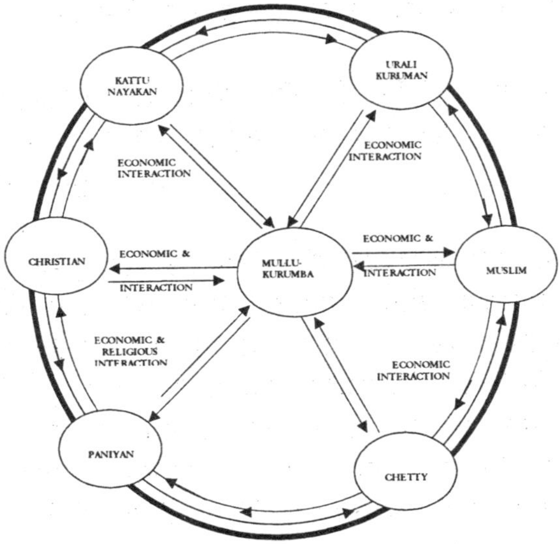

Figure 4: Social Interaction during 1960s

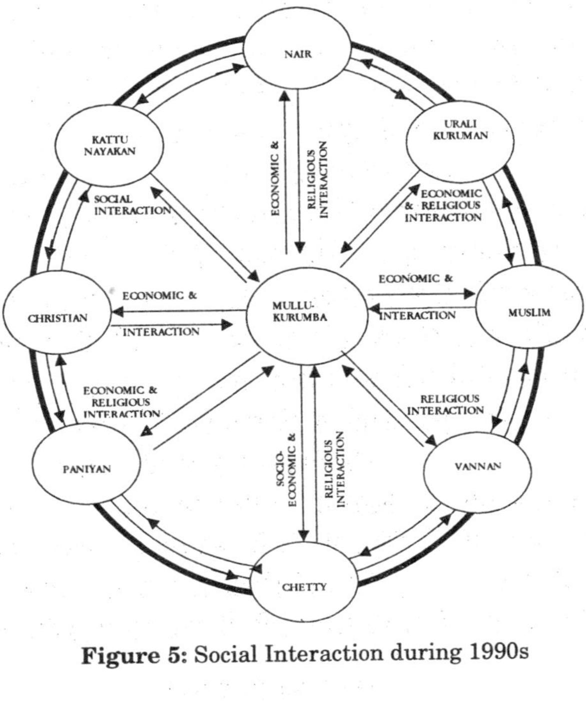

Figure 5: Social Interaction during 1990s

The Chetty, considered as a low caste Hindu group, now became numerically dominant in this region and have economic and socio-religious interaction with the Mullukurumba. Mullukurumba also have economic and religious interaction with the Nairs. Another caste that comes in close contact with the Mullukurumba is the Vannan, who attend birth, marriage and death and provide ritual service to the Mullukurumba and in return they are paid in cash.

Borrowing of money at an exorbitant rate, mortgage and selling of land are the direct results of the interaction of Mullukurumba with the Christian, and most of their lands were encroached by these in-migrant Christians. The Mullukurumba learned wetland cultivation of tapioca, foot-yam, ginger, banana etc., from Christians. Contact with the in-migrants like Christian and Muslim brought the Mullukurumba community more closely to the market economy.

Chapter - 6

DISCUSSION

The different aspects of the Mullukurumba life and culture detailed in the foregoing chapters are examined here in the light of various theories relating to socio-cultural changes, in the context of tribal situation in India.

In India, though in the past, the tribes inhabited the isolated geographical areas; they never lived in complete isolation. Some how or other, they maintained casual contacts with the population living around them including those inhabiting the plains. And it is a fact that no culture can be static forever. Haimendorf (1977:1) commented that:

> " For thousands of years, primitive tribes persisted in forests and hills without having more than casual contacts with the population of the open plains and the centres of civilization. Now and then, a military campaign extending for a short spell into the vastness of tribal country would bring the inhabitants temporarily to the notice of Princess and chronicles, but for long periods there was frictionless co-existence between the tribal folks and Hindu castes in the society in the truest sense of the world" (cf. Pasayath, 1998:103).

According to Aiyappan (1988:17), "the Proto-Australoid and Mediterranean strains have been living together for so many thousands of years, and the racial difference between them was so very slight, that racial admixture between them has been going on without serious obstacles, with the result that pure Proto-Mediterraneans and pure Proto-Australoids are now mostly stastitical abstractions".

The invasion of tribal territories by the people of the plains, for various purposes commenced during the colonial era and was intensified during the post-colonial period (Tharakan 1978). These contacts brought about significant changes in the tribal areas in the form of development activities, urbanisation, introduction of markets, spread of education etc., and also accelerated the processes of culture contact, acculturation and assimilation (Mencher 1975: 130; Kurup 1988: 158). The Mullukurumba were not free from such courses of action.

Gudalur taluk of Nilgiri district, where the Mullukurumba inhabits, was a part of Madras State until the reorganization of States in 1956, and this area was then included in the Wayanad taluk of the erst-while Malabar district (Logan 1887). Aiyappan while examining the situation during the pre-British period argues:

> "The Wynad taluk is geographically a part of the Nilgiri plateau. The eastern half of Wynad contiguous with the Nilgiris and Coorg is inhabited by Kanara speaking tribes. When the Nilgiri-Wynad plateau began to be opened up by European planters, they found the country in the possession of a few landlords, chiefly Malayalees for, the whole of the Wynad area, until its cession to the East India Company by Tippu Sultan was part of the dominions of the Raja of Kottayam. The actual cultivators were the tribes, such as the Kurichiyas, Mulla Kurumbar and Chettis" (1948: 92).

Rajalakshmi Misra (1971:3) recollects the past in the following words:

> "Erumad village, which is a part of the erstwhile Wynad taluk of Malabar, was amidst thick jungle till about three decades ago and was the abode of wild animals. The Mullukurumbas and the other tribes of this village and of neighbourhood had slain a tiger in Erumad only twenty years ago. Now, though the hillocks are still covered with thick green vegetation, the wild animals have vanished".

The above accounts give a clear picture of the Mullukurumba habitat during pre-British period. Prior to the arrival of European planters, this area was possessed by a few landlords like Kuppathode Nairs and cultivation of land was done by the Chettis and the tribes including the Mullukurumba and Kurichiyan (Logan 1887, Thurston 1909, Aiyappan 1982). Again, this area had been a thick forest with wild animals. Denudation of forests was started with the arrival of non-tribes from the various parts of the country. In modern history of Kerala, the migration of peasant communities of Travancore, from rural to rural regions took place at two occasions; the first instance was from 1850s to early 1900s and then the second from 1930s to 1960s (Kurup 1988: 51). The in-migration of large-scale population from various parts of Kerala to Wayanad area during 1941-71 had resulted in the population growth by leaps and bounds during this period (Tharakan 1978; Kurup 1988). The situation of Kappala during 1960s, according to Rajalakshmi Misra (1971:4) is as follows:

> "There has been a continuous flow of the population from Kerala-specially that of the Christians and the Moplas settling down in Erumad village. The latter have monopolized the trade while the former agriculture, in Erumad village. Tamil speaking ex-servicemen (Harijan) have been allotted plots of land here by the Madras Government to settle down, and a separate settlement of these people has come up in this village. The native Chettis living in this village however continue to be the more prosperous people of this area"

Thus, the flow of various communities to Nilgiri–Wayanad transformed this area into a multi-ethnic region and these caste and communities slowly started interacting and influencing the life of natives, especially, the Mullukurumba. The nature of influence was not one-sided, but a two-way process of interaction and influence leading to a multi-dimentional disposition.

Prior to the arrival of migrants, the Mullukurumba economy was characterised by hunting, gathering and shifting cultivation. Since most of their day-to-day life activities were centered on the forest, the ecological (geographical) factors played an important role in shaping their way of life. This aspect has been further elaborated by Singh (1987: 312) and Netting (1971:24) as follows:

> "Geographical conditions or factors are those that influence the human life and they are free from human control. All the characteristics that are found in man and the society are the result of the geographical factors. Distribution of population on land, racial conflict, economic, political, religious organization and their nature, progress and downfall of civilization etc., are all caused by the geographical factors. Geographical factors that influence the human life and behaviour are also responsible for the changes in it".

Here, the geographical factors like favourable climatic condition, high fertility of soil etc., of this region influenced the colonial planters (Logan 1887), who later paved the way for the large scale in-migration of non-tribes, resulting 'the closure and creation of niches', as pointed out by Gadgil and Guha (1992:242-243).

> "In India, the British usurped the ecological niches occupied by the hunter-gatherers, many of whom also practiced shifting cultivation, and diminished substantially the niche space occupied by food producers, by alienating them from access to non-cultivated lands. The tremendous shrinkage of the niche-space available to the Indian population was only marginally compensated by new niches. The collaborators in the formation of new niches prospered as time went by, the others - hunters, gatherers, peasants, artisans and pastoral and non-pastoral nomads- had all to squeeze into the already diminishing niche-space for food production" (cf: Kulirani 1996:196-97).

The non-tribes' activities such as clearing of forests for housing, farming etc., diminished the niche or shared space (Godelier 1978: 404, Sack 1986: 19, Wargo 1988, Beach & Anderson 1992: 62, Rao 1992:95, Barnad 1992: 146) occupied by the Mullukurumba, who had a strong subsistence base of wetland paddy cultivation, shifting cultivation, hunting, fishing and animal husbandry. Satisfying the subsistence needs, rather than increasing the quantity of production, dominated the Mullukurumba producers. They did not bother about occupying large tracts of forest land, as personal possessions, because they did not attach themselves with dry-land due to the practice of shifting cultivation (Francis: 1996:173-174). This reiterates the theoretical stand with respect to cultural adaptation taken by Sahalins (1972) as "the more adapted a culture, the less therefore it is adaptable".

The system of communal *pattayam* in the name of *porunnavan* existed in this community prior to the commencement of individual *pattayam* in 1964, which consecutively resulted in private ownership of property. Thus, the problem of holding and managing uneconomic small holdings of individual land, in other words, diminishing of the niche space (Wargo 1988), made the Mullukurumba to adapt with the changing situation by slowly adopting the economic activities of the in-migrants, who possessed superior agricultural technologies compared to that of their subsistence economy (Kurup: 1988, Kulirani: 1996).

During pre-migration period, the Chettis dominated the economic scene in Nilgiri-Wayanad. The Mullukurumba maintained social status just below the Chettis. They worked on the fields of Chettis, along with Kattunayakan and Paniyan. Kattunayakan and Paniyan were also worked in the fields of Mullukurumba. The Uralikuruman supplied implements to these communities. Thus, all these natives kept a kind of socio-economic and ritual ties amongst themselves. The situation has changed owing to the urbanisation of the area as a result of large-scale in-migration of land hungry peasants. In India, the growth of urban population in the predominantly tribal area has increased specially after the second global war (Vidyarthi & Rai: 1976). Here also, in-migration started during 1940s and the in-migrant communities having different subsistence activities with superior technologies, made the area urban.

Urbanisation accelerated the realm of the interaction of Mullukurumba with other communities and thereby, brought changes in their way of life, especially in the economic sphere. Smailes (1975) defines urbanisation as a "process whereby land and inhabitants becomes urban. It refers to a change in both place and people....Urbanisation means that an increasing proportion of human society becomes townsfolk, and as this happens, towns grow in population, spread in area, and make an ever-increasing impact upon the countryside, both upon its appearance and upon the life of its inhabitants. More and more of the landscape becomes townscape, and people come to live in an environment that is both physically and socially urban" (cited in Maheswari Prasad 1980:90). Urbanisation has led to cultural change by providing ways and means to improve the cultural standards of living (Agarwal 1977: 138, Pasayath 1998). Aurora also discusses the influences of urban centres on the socio-cultural, economic and political processes of tribal India who are not exactly part and parcel of the dominant culture of the region, but lie on the periphery (cited in Bhandari 1980:73).

Urbanisation enhanced market economy and the in-migrants such as the Christians and Muslims have monopolized the agriculture and the trade respectively (Rajalakshmi Misra 1971). Opening of market and monopoly of trade by the in-migrant Muslims demanded more cash crops from the region, and it is reflected in the economic activities of the Mullukurumba too. The Mullukurumba who were contented with the subsistence cultivation, in the past, have now started growing various cash crops. Those who were reluctant to do cash crops cultivation, either gave their land to the migrants for lease or sold their land, as an adaptive strategy. Moreover, the Mullukurumba who lost their major portion of land, were compelled to work in their own land as hired labourers for low wages. This reaffirms the view that the cultures act as selection forces upon one another, and progress is viewed as an outcome of adaptation and selection (Sahlins 1965).

Thus, increasing labour demands in the village on account of intensive agricultural activities added with deforestation, prohibition of commercial exploitation of forest, restrictions imposed on shifting cultivation, Land Reforms Act etc., forced the Mullukurumba to join the labour market. In short, contact with the non-tribes brought the Mullukurumba more close to the market economy. The changes in the traditional tribal economies of the Mullukurumba due to continuous contact with the neighbouring castes and urbanisation are not different from other similar situations explained by other scholars who worked on the tribal economies of other areas (e.g. Hutton 1935, Ghurye 1943, Bailey 1961, Kosambi 1965, Bose 1971, Aurora 1972, Misra 1977, Kulirani 1982, Hazra 1983, Vidyarthi and Rai 1985, Furer-Haimendorf 1985, Bhanu 1989, Nayak 1990, Choudhury 1992, Rizvi 1994, 1996, Devarapalli 1996, Sasikumar 1997).

It is observed that the traditional economies of the Mullukurumba and other tribal communities, which had a symbiotic character, have given way to a market economy. They are now totally depending on the market for all essential commodities. The customary labour relations have, by and large, given way to wages paid in cash (Kulirani 1982, 1996). Thus, the urban impact is visible in increase of income, improvement in the standard of living and change in the attitude pattern. The impact of urbanisation on the Mullukurumba cultural fabric is clearly evident from the infrastructure facilities available to them, when compared to the situation almost half-a-century ago as explained by Rajalakshmi Misra (1971:3, 1972), Misra (1977), Kulirani (1982: 11) and Tharakan and Bhanu (1994: 98).

Although the areas where the Mullukurumba inhabits have become urbanized and flourished, it does not indicate the degree of development of Mullukurumba, as cautioned by Sharma (1976: 2), who notes, "The regional development may not be an indicator of tribal development in the region. It is quite possible to visualize a situation where a tribal community may not at all be benefited even though the indicators of development may show a continuous upward trend.... Study of growth centre in tribal setting thus has to examine how far the local output increase has been beneficial to the tribal economies". It is a fact that regional development and emergence of township or market had its positive and negative influence on the Mullukurumba (Kulirani 1982: 11). At the positive side, some of them are able to participate in the development process; while on the negative side, it created a class cleavage i.e., a class of privileged and another of under privileged. A similar situation has been reported among the Kanikkar of Thiruvananthapuram by Sasikumar (1997: 224). The under privileged are part of growing labour market (Kulirani 1982: 10, 1996: 181). The under privileged status or backwardness is not due to cultural reasons, but it is the product of the colonial and neocolonial exploitation (Pathy: 1987).

Now, the Mullukurumba economy represents a complex system, i.e., a combination of the economic activities of their own and that of the in-migrants' as well (Tharakan and Bhanu 1994: 99). Bailey (1958: 228) opined that when a relatively simple peasant economy or tribal economy is brought into contact with modern world, as a result of the interaction of the two systems, a third complex system emerges. This is in agreement with the position taken by Levi-Strauss (1963) on social change, as "a shift in one of the parts or component of social structure will result in the total transformation of social structure". The changed complex economic system is found to be more dependent on other social systems in terms of a cash economy. In addition to this, heterogeneity in social interaction, social stratification and the diversification of network of relations shows that the Mullukurumbas are moving away from the tribal end of the 'tribe- peasant and tribe-caste continuum' proposed by Sinha (1953, 1958, 1962, 1965), Bailey (1960), Bose (1971) and Madelbaum (1989). The situation found among the Mullukurumba cannot be conceived as the 'Hindu method of tribal absorption' a theory proposed by N.K. Bose for the culture change among the tribes of Northern India

(Bose 1971). Redfield also maintains a similar position when he generalizes about the absorption of the 'little tradition by the great tradition' (Redfield 1934). The above theories are applicable to the end products of change, and it necessarily does not narrate the process of culture change. It explains the direction of mobility due to the power or pulls exerted on the tribal cultures by the dominant caste Hindus. The Caste Hindus under the broader term Huinduism did not consider the tribes as a part of 'Brahminical Hinduism' earlier or even today. The culture change happening among the Mullukurumba is in the opposite direction, and it is still a process of change induced from within and not from outside. It suggests neither the beginning nor the end; it reveals an ongoing process of culture change just initiated within. The change is not initiated or induced by the neighbouring dominant Caste Hindus, but the tribes themselves initiate it. It is, therefore, to be understood as the 'tribal mode of Hindu absorption' rather than the Hindu method of tribal absorption. This is explicit from the statement of Sinha, who says, "Even the upper levels of tribes, such as the Bhumiji, Munda and Gond, established their claims to be Kshtriyas" (Sinha 1962). It is the claim of the tribes, which has come from them and, it is not a status imposed on them by the Caste Hinhus. It is to be understood from the position of the tribes rather than from the point of view of the researcher. Had Sinha (1953, 1958, 1962, 1965) and Bose (1971) given importance to the emic view, they would not have come to the earlier generalizations.

Further, a new system of economy has emerged out of culture contact along with urbanisation. Development programmes had its impact on the other aspects of the social systems as well. Those who had earned better income from plantation works, and those who got better education and well placed, showed a tendency to move away from their traditional settlements. The breaking down of communal living enhanced the neolocal residence pattern as against their traditional patrilocal residence pattern (Tharakan and Bhanu 1994: 99). Shrinkage of ecological niche had its impact on food resources, dietary habits, and health seeking behaviour, pattern of interaction with other tribes and non-tribes and power blocks. Further, the disappearance of tribal self-sufficiency and culture contact has led to the decline of tribal reciprocal obligations. Money has great influence among them. In other words, cash cropping, though strengthened the individual enterprises, it weakened the cooperation of households at *veedu* level (Rajalakshmi Misra 1971, Kulirani 1982, Tharakan and Bhanu 1994: 100). High rate of external contact and present social condition disturbed their traditional religious system and the power of the Mullukurumba political organisation. Now, the Mullukurumba political system consists of a mixture of both traditional and contemporary forms. But, there is little change in their family structure, authority, rights and inheritance pattern, proving the fact that development brings changes only in some aspects of social structure while other elements of culture remained the same (Bailey 1958, Kulirani 1982, Pathy 1987, Tharakan and Bhanu 1994, Sasikumar 1997).

Again, educated and employed showed inclination to improve their status, which is reflected in the adoption of names that do not reveal the tribal status. Many of them started adopting names, which are popular with the Caste Hindus. In a similar study, besides other things, Furer-Haimendorf had noted similar attitudinal changes among the Reddis (1985: 271-72). More over, there observed a cultural and structural continuum between the tribes and lower caste Hindus (Sinha 1959, Tharakan and Bhanu 1994).

The close contacts and co-existence between the tribes and Caste Hindus over a prolonged period have paved the way for rapid cultural interaction in Gudallur and Wayanad. Interaction may be primarily in relation to economic activities and religion, finally leading to 'Hinduisation' of tribes (Aurora: 1972, Tharakan and Bhanu 1994). Ghurye (1943, 1959) has outlined the natural process of 'assimilation' of tribes, so far Hinduized, that they have got assimilated as different castes in the caste system.

The appearance of religious elements of the Caste Hindu like–worship of Hindu gods along with their own deities, visiting Hindu pilgrim centers, making offerings, observing fast, giving sacredness to ossimum plant, celebrating Hindu festivals, celebration of the regional festival (*puthari)*, sprinkling holy water (*punniyaham*) on mother and child, recording the date of birth and birth star of newborns, adopting popular Caste Hindu names, conducting first hair cutting, first rice feeding, marriage in temples with the participation of outsiders, etc.,–in the day-to-day life of the Mullukurumba reveal the nature and process of cultural adaptation by adopting cultural elements from the dominant caste Hindus. The adoption of cultural elements from the caste Hindus or 'Hinduism' also makes the presence of Brahmin priests inevitable, which in turn weakens the authority and dignity of the traditional political leader (*porunnavan*). According to Singh, (1994: 12) religion has been the continuance of the autonomy of the tribal religious system in spite of the tribes' close interaction with Christianity and Hinduism. Although the Mullukurumba had close economic ties with Christians, impact of Christianity has been felt least among the Mullukurumba, unlike the tribal communities of the other parts of the country, especially in middle India (Roy 1928, Sahay 1963, Sachchidanand 1964, Vidyarthi and Rai 1985) or South India.

There are numerous tribes (or sections), which have undergone acculturation and have adopted selected traits or features of the regional Hindusim to their traditional cultures, like–the concept of purity and pollution, observing Hindu festivals, worshipping Hindu Gods, Hindu way of observing life cycle rites, adopting Hindu caste surnames, etc., (Srivastava 1958, Sinha 1959, Majumdar 1962, Sahay 1962, Sachchidanand 1964, Sen Gupta 1969, Vidyarthi 1966, Tharakan and Bhanu 1994.

No known society is free from the tides of change. As far as the Mullukurumba are concerned, they keep adjusting with other neighbouring groups and at times make fundamental changes in order to get acceptance in other cultural traditions resulting 'composite societies' or 'plural societies' (Radcliffe-Brown 1952).

To quote Redfield (1941:xiv), "In Yucatan, as you pass from village to town, or from town to city, you find some elements of living that you left behind. Only they are differently accented, differently worked into the whole of the local life. So the differences are not like those among the paint tablets in a paint box; they are like the colours of a spectrum". The Mullukurumba too have become a part of the wider plural society. Their material culture and certain aspects of their way of life are found to be similar to the neighbouring communities (Tharakan and Bhanu 1994: 98). It is like a continuum. "Continuum refers to an uninterrupted series of gradual changes in the magnitude of a given characteristic, forming a linear increase or decrease (Pasayat 1998: 276-277).

But, in spite of all these changes, certain areas of the traditional culture of Mullukurumba, like principles of monogamy, tribal endogamy, clan exogamy, ancestral worship etc., still remain unaltered. The traditional political system also persists with the essential modifications that have become necessary. In this context the observation of Lancy (Census of India 1931), "An aboriginal will adopt certain Hindu customs, he will join in certain Hindu procession, he may even make offerings to certain Hindu deities, and at the same time he may adhere in the main to his old tribal belief and practices" is found to be still relevant. Thus, we may conclude that, although the Mullukurumba community is undergoing transformation by adopting cultural traits or elements from the local socio-economic systems, their core culture remains intact. It is possible because the transformation among them is from within. Change is through selection and leading to adaptation. Thus, we conclude that the culture change among the Mullukurumba is generalized as a tribal mode of Hindu absorption rather than the Hindu method of tribal absorption.

ANNEXURE - 1

Table 1
Hunting groups and Hunting areas

Sl. No.	*Name of settlement*	*Types of inter-group alliance in Big Games*	*Forest Areas assigned to the Group for Big Games*
1.	Nedungode	1, 2	Meenmutti, an extension of Nadukani
2.	Kappala	2, 1	-do-
3.	Theyyakkuni	3, 4, 5, 6	Cherambadi
4.	Onimoola	4, 3, 5, 6	-do-
5.	Narivallapu	5, 6, 4, 3	-do-
6.	Kappikkunnu	6, 5, 4, 3	-do-
7.	Kallichal	7, 8, 9, 10	Cherangod
8.	Padicheri	8, 7, 9, 10	-do-
9.	Konnatu	9,7, 8, 10	-do-
10.	Madakkundu	10, 9, 8, 7	-do-
11.	Tharavarakkolli		

Source: Based on the data collected in 1990 by staff and students of the Department of Anthropology. The fieldwork was done for the preparation of dissertations as part of the M. A. Degree course in Anthropology. Dr. B. Ananda Bhanu and Dr. Vineetha Menon supervised the fieldwork and edited the dissertations.

ANNEXURE - 2

Table 2
Plant Foods

Sl. No.	*Name of the Forest Resource*	*Type of plant*	*Available Months*
1.	Nura	Creepers	August & September
2.	Nara		All months
3.	Korama		Januaray
4.	Perum kuman	Mushrooms	June to September
5.	Katu potian		
6.	Nedum taly		
7.	Ambum kuman		
8.	Nakkuman		
9.	Valakuman		
10.	Pithukuman		
11.	Vellaramkuman		
12.	Pazha cheera	Leaves	
13.	Chokanna cheera		December to May
14.	Kozhi cheera		
15.	Mutinga chappu		All Months
16.	Payar chappu		
17.	Ponnam kanny		June to September
18.	Chembin tal		
19.	Avara	Bean varieties	June, July
20.	Katan kozhy		
21.	Mavavara		
22.	Vilachi payar		August, September
23.	Posha payar		
24.	Tatta payar		
25.	Tukayavara		
26.	Neyyavara		
27.	Achili	Fruits	March & April
28.	Ngaval		March & April
29.	Choori		April & May
30.	Kodita		May & June
31.	Pollanga		May & June
32.	Kara		June & July

Source: Based on the data collected in 1990 by staff and students of the Department of Anthropology. The fieldwork was done for the preparation of dissertations as part of the M. A. Degree course in Anthropology. Dr. B. Ananda Bhanu and Dr. Vineetha Menon supervised the fieldwork and edited the dissertations.

ANNEXURE - 3

Table 3
Agricultural Produces

Sl. No.	*Name of the Agri. Produces*	*Available Months*	*Nature of Use*
1.	Banana	All months	Self consumption,
2.	Tapioca	-do-	Reciprocal exchange
3.	Sweet potato		& cash crop
4.	Cucumber		
5.	Elephant yam	August,	Self consumption &
6.	Brinjal	September	Reciprocal exchange
7.	Bean varieties		
8.	Coffee	December-February	
9.	Pepper	February-March	Self consumption,
10.	Turmeric	November	Reciprocal exchange
11.	Ginger	January, June & July	& cash crop
12.	Paddy	November	
13.	Tomato	Rainy season	

Source: Based on the data collected in 1990 by staff and students of the Department of Anthropology. The fieldwork was done for the preparation of dissertations as part of the M. A. Degree course in Anthropology. Dr. B. Ananda Bhanu and Dr. Vineetha Menon supervised the fieldwork and edited the dissertations.

ANNEXURE - 4

Table 4
Kinship Terms

Sl. No.	*Relationship*	*Term of Reference*	*Term of Address*
1.	Ego's Father	*Achan*	*Acha*
2.	Ego's Mother	*Amma*	*Amma / Amme*
3.	Father's father/Mother's father	*Muttappan*	*Muttappa*
4.	Father's mother/ Mother's mother	*Muttamma*	*Muttamma / Muttamme*
5.	Father's elder brother mother's elder sister's husband	*Peyappan*	*Peyappa*
6.	Father's younger brother Mother's younger sister's husband	*Eyappan*	*Eyappa*
7.	Father's elder brother's wife mother's elder sister	*Peymma*	*Peymme*
8.	Father's younger brother's wifeMother's younger sister	*Eyamma*	*Eyamme*
9.	Mother's brother's wife Mother-in-law	*Ammayi*	*Ammayi*
10.	Father's younger sister	*Mami*	*Mami*
11.	Father's elder sister's husband	*Maman*	*Mama*
12.	Elder brother	*Annan*	*Anna*
13.	Elder brother's wife	*Periyol*	*Periyole*
14.	Younger brother	*Aniyan*	*Aniya*
15.	Younger brother's wife	*Cheriyol*	*Cheriyole*
16.	Elder sister	*Etta*	*Etta*
17.	Younger sister	*Aniyathi*	*Aniyathi*
18.	Sister's husband wife's brother	*Aliyan*	*Aliya*
19.	Husband's elder brother	*Periavar*	*Periavare*
20.	Husband's sister	*Nathun*	*Nathune*
21.	Son	*Makan*	*Makane / Mone*
22.	Daughter	*Makal*	*Makale / Mole*
23.	Son's sonDaughter's son	*Motten*	*Motta*
24.	Son's daughterDaughter's daughter	*Mottathi*	*Mottathi*

Source: Based on the data collected in 1990 by staff and students of the Department of Anthropology. The fieldwork was done for the preparation of dissertations as part of the M.A. Degree course in Anthropology. Dr. B. Ananda Bhanu and Dr. Vineetha Menon supervised the fieldwork and edited the dissertations.

ANNEXURE - 5-A

Development programmes undertaken by the Government

I. Health

There is a Public Health Centre at Kappala. The inhabitants of the neighbouring settlements like, Nedungode, Theyyakkuni and Onimoola depend on this PHC. Usually immunisation camps are conducted in this PHC. In Kappala settlement, the Panchayath had constructed latrines in 1980. But the people could not make use of them owing to the non-availability of water.

II. Education

Adi Dravida and Tribal Welfare Department had constructed a Government Tribal Residential School (GTRS) in Kappala in 1964. Here, classes are conducted from 1st standard to 8th standard. Students' strength in this school in 1990 was 250, out of which 75 children were from Kappala. The number of teachers in this school in 1990 was only four. Even though food and accommodation are provided to the students, they are not interested in utilizing the residential facilities. Since, Nedungode settlement is situated near the Kappala settlement; the children from here also attend GTRS in Kappala. Children from Theyyakkuni, Onimoola, Kappikkunnu and Narivalappu settlements either attend GTRS, Kappala or go to Erumadu School. A 'Children Welfare Centre' established by the Social Welfare Department, functions adjacent to the GTRS. Almost 17 children from the Kappala settlement were going there in 1990. Adult Education programmes were undertaken in this area since 1987-88.

III. Occupation

In 1985, two persons of Kappala got training at the State Institute of Rural Development at Bhavani Sagar under TRYSEM. But they could not secure any job after training. Forest Department appointed two persons for plant sapling and they were given Rs. 300/-, and 30kg rice and wheat monthly. But after five months, the Department ceased the same without any reason.

In Theyyakkuni, a self-employment programme of Eucalyptus distillery sponsored by the Central Govt. was started in 1986 and the person who was entrusted to do this work was given loan from the Khadi Board to build distilling sheds. After building shed, the board gave distilling apparatus made of brass at free of cost. In 1990, it was found that a non-tribe claims the ownership of this distillery. The Mullukurumba had given this distillery to this non-tribe for a rent of Rs. 3000 per year.

In October 1989, the Syndicate Bank of Erumadu adopted Narivallapu settlement under a scheme called 'Sampoorna Scheme'. But no loan was given till February1990. Among the Mullukurumba, almost 15 persons secured job in various State and Central Government Departments.

IV. Agriculture

Only one person from Kappala settlement got agricultural loan of Rs. 2000/- at 10% interest from Canara Bank in 1988 and he utilized it for agricultural works in his own fields. Another person from Theyyakkuni got a loan of Rs. 5000/- for agricultural purpose from the Co-operative Society, Erumadu in 1988. Except these two settlements, no other settlements got any loan relating to agriculture till 1990.

V. Animal Husbandry

In the case of Kappala settlement, a man got a buffalo free of cost in 1984. In 1985-86, the Govt. has launched a scheme to supply milch cows and this was supplied through the Canara Bank of Cherambadi. At first they selected 15 persons from Kappala and gave an amount of Rs. 18000/- to them as advance to make cowsheds. But later officials gave only 3 milch cows as a joint ownership to 15 persons. Thus, 15 persons became indebted to the Canara Bank for 3 milch cows

In Nedungode settlement, two persons got a loan of Rs. 2000/- each with a subsidy of Rs. 600/- from the Canara Bank in 1986-87 to buy plough bulls. Like wise, in Theyyakkuni also, a man got a loan of Rs. 2000/- with a subsidy of Rs. 800/- from the Syndicate Bank, Erumadu in 1986-87 to buy plough bulls.

VI. Infrastructure

(i) Housing

In 1952, Rs.700/- each was given to three persons in Kappala settlement for house construction, without any subsidy. The inhabitants built three houses each in Kappikkunnu and Narivallapu without any help from external agencies.

(ii) Drinking Water

During 1954- 1968, the Adi Dravida and Tribal Welfare Department constructed wells in Kappala (1968), Nedungode (1954), Theyyakkuni, Kappikkunnu and Narivallapu. In addition to this, the panchayath provided pipe water in Kappala, Onimoola, Kappikkunnu and Narivallapu.

(iii) Communication (Road)

In 1968, Adi Dravida and Tribal Welfare Department had constructed footpath from main road to the two settlements viz., Kappala and Nedungode. In Narivallapu, the Panchayath constructed a link road from the main road to the settlement. But in Theyyakkuni and Onimoola, the inhabitants themselves constructed a link road from the main road to their settlements. Now, all the settlements have been connected by tarred road. To make the communication network functional, a few approach roads and footpaths have also been laid in a few settlements across agricultural fields.

(iv) Electricity

Electricity is available in the following settlements viz., Kappala, Nedungode, Theyyakkuni, Onimoola, Kappikkunnu and Narivallapu.

ANNEXURE-5-B

Development programmes undertaken by the Voluntary Organizations

The voluntary organizations play a vital role in the development of a society. In the case of Mullukurumba too, the role of such organizations is significant. The voluntary organizations working among the Mullukurumba include: ACCORD (Action for Community Organizations, Rehabilitation and Development), AMS (Adivasi Munneta Sangham),Adivasi Women's Sangham, NAWA (Nilgiri Adivasi Welfare Association),AKIMS (Adivasi Kurumba Ilaigner Munneta Sangham) and BAJSS (Bharathiya Adimajathi Sevak Sangh)

ACCORD (Action for Community Organizations, Rehabilitation & Development)

The main objective of ACCORD, which started functioning in 1986, was to uplift the tribes. Its office is located in Gudallur taluk and operates with the financial aid from both government and other agencies. Members in this organization include tribes and non-tribes as well. The number of tribal members in this organization in 1990 was 52. This organization concentrates mainly on the uplift of the tribes by giving aid for their agricultural activities, providing health facilities, aid for construction of houses and also in the field of education.

Agriculture

ACCORD gives due importance to the development of agriculture among the Mullukurumba and planned scheme for cultivation of tea, pepper etc. For this purpose, this organization has given training to a few selected Mullukurumba in tea plantation. After the training, they were given practical experience in tea plantation. These trained people in turn gave training in tea plantation to their people in the concerned settlements. ACCORD initially distributed tea plants and fertilizers at free of cost. But, at the time of plucking leaves, the tribes had to pay 30 paise each per tea plant. Each tea plant costs one rupees in the open market.

In Kallichal settlement, almost eight acres of land had been utilized for tea plantation. Almost thirty-five Mullukurumba had cultivated tea in their land and yielded result. This result attracted more and more Mullukurumba to take up plantation activities. ACCORD has received 250 applications till December 1989.

Poultry

Another scheme of ACCORD is supplying poultry to the tribals. ACCORD bought best kind of hens named *Giriraja*, from Bangalore and supplied four to five hens at free of cost to all families. Kappala and Kallichal are the two settlements benefited under this scheme.

Health

Health status of the Nilgiri tribes is very poor compared to the tribes of Wayanad. Though they suffer from several kinds of diseases, least care was given to their health. Under the label of ACCORD, two doctors visited the tribal settlements periodically and treated them. Doctors also took class on cleanliness and prevention of diseases. There was a team of trained tribes, who worked as assistants to these doctors, and visited each settlement and supplied medicines after examining the patients free of cost.

Education

The tribals were unaware of the importance of education. Though a Balavadi was started at Theyyakuni in 1988, the number of children was only 12. The classes were from 10.00 a.m to 12.30 p.m. The teacher belonged to Mullukurumba community and hailed from Theyyakuni settlement. In some of the settlements, Mullukurumba got adult education through ACCORD. ACCORD had a plan to open Model School (School of learning) for the tribes. For this purpose, they proposed an education pattern giving importance to tribal culture.

Housing

ACCORD also had plans for house construction for Mullukurumba and gave them training in building works. Six men got training in house construction. In 1989, ACCORD built two houses at Kozhikolly. ACCORD has appointed five Mullukurumba men (three from Kappala and two from Theyyakuni settlements) as social workers with a monthly honorarium of Rs. 500/-.

There are some other organizations under ACCORD with an aim to help tribes to solve their problems. The Adivasi Munneta Sangham (AMS) and the Adivasi Women's Sangham are main organization in this area.

AMS (Adivasi Munneta Sangham)

This Sangham started functioning in 1988 and Subramani, a resident of Kappala settlement was the president in 1989. The aims of this organization are given below:

1. All adivasi who are above eighteen years of age must be given land not less than 3 acres;
2. To reclaim the alienated land;
3. To get laws enacted to prevent Adivasi from alienating their land to non-tribes.
4. To claim back land from the Reserve forest for their burial ground;
5. To get a Special Tribal Officer appointed in the taluk for solving their land problems.

There was a special 'Adivasi Credit Fund' programme started under the AMS. Under this programme, each member has to deposit Rs. 5/- in this fund. The money, thus collected, is deposited in the joint account of the Sangham President and the Sangham Treasurer at the Syndicate Bank. If any member needed a loan, amount would be given with an interest of 5 per cent per hundred rupees. They also conduct cultural programmes under the leadership of the AMS, which helps them to preserve their cultural heritage.

Adivasi Women's Sangham

Women's association in each settlement is known by the name of the settlement. This Sangham started functioning in 1987 in order to eliminate the social evil like-alcoholism among the tribes. In1987, the Sangham started propaganda against this social evil under the leadership of two Mullukurumba women named Ramadevi and Devaki. They captured all the arrack centres of the areas and cracked them. Thus, the beginning of the Womens' Sangham was a big sensation in the area.

After this event, they received more encouragement from both ACCORD and other tribal settlements. The Sangham conducted orientation classes to the tribal women and made them more conscious of the world around them. They discussed the importance of health and prevention of diseases etc. The Mullukurumba do not like to use vegetables. The women's Sangham made a campaign against this by illustrating the need to include vegetables in their diet. They also organized a campaign to demonstrate the value of traditional treatment and the problems, particularly side effects of allopathic medicines.

The women's Sangham started a saving deposit scheme in October 1988. Each member of this Sangham was directed to deposit a monthly amount of Rs. 2/- and a 'nazhi' rice (350 gm.). Rice was sold to the needy and the amount was deposited in the savings account. Money was returned with an interest of 5 percent for every hundred rupees. Thus, the sangham tried to improve the economic status of the Mullukurumba. They also helped poor Mullukurumba in house construction and at the time of their agricultural operations as well.

NAWA (Nilgiri Adivasi Welfare Association)

NAWA is a voluntary, secular and charitable organization solely concerned with the welfare activities among the tribes in Nilgiri district and adjoining areas. This association was registered in 1958 under the Society Act of 1860 and affiliated to the Bharathiya Adimajathi Sevak Sangh, New Delhi. This association concentrated mainly on the health, education and socio-economic development of the tribes. Dr. S. Narasinhan, a doctor, who felt that there was great need to work among the forgotten Nilgiri tribes and began working for them as early as 1940's. He was the founder of this organization. The main works of this organization are as follows:

Child Sponsorship Programme

The NAWA gave priority for the development of education among the tribes. For this, NAWA adopted one child from each family and took the entire responsibility of their education. Beside, NAWA deposited an amount in the name of the adopted children in such a way that they could withdraw the amount after the completion of their studies. Kappala, Theyyakuni, Kallichal and Nedungodu settlements have been benefited from this programme. Since the parents had no burden in educating their children thus adopted, the tribes were happy about this scheme.

Health

Another programme of NAWA was in the field of health. A hospital at Pothukolly near Kayyunni was opened by this organization, where the tribes got free treatment. Health workers used to visit houses of tribes and gave instructions and made them aware of the importance of maintaining health. Beside this, they also gave financial aid to the tribes at the time of agricultural operations and house construction. At Kappala, a community hall was built by this organization.

AKIMS (Adivasi Kurumba Ilaigner Munneta Sangham)

This was the first organization that started among the Mullukurumba. It was registered in 1979. Initially its aim was to uplift the Mullukurumba. Later they expanded their area of activities to other tribes and named it as AKIMS (Adivasi Kurumba Illeigner Munneta Sangham). This is a youth organization. It functions at Cherangodu panchayat.

This organization gave economic assistance for medical treatment, house construction, agricultural operations etc. Members of AKIMS by way of their labour, free of wages, constructed a house at Onimoola.

This organization also aims to prevent land alienation. At Tharavarakolly there was a land alienation case, which was settled peacefully with the intervention of AKIMS. They built a link road from the Nedungodu settlement to the Erumadu-Manalvayal road. Due to lack of funds they could not do any major work.

BAJSS (Bharathiya Adima Jathi Sevak Sangh)

BAJSS set up crèche in tribal areas. The crèche functions at Kallichal had 25 children below the age group of three years, in the year 1990. Children were given free vegetable meals. A teacher and a maid (from Kallichal settlement) were employed in this crèche.

Source

Based on the data collected in 1990 by staff and students of the Department of Anthropology. The fieldwork was done for the preparation of dissertations as part of the M.A. Degree course in Anthropology. Dr. B. Ananda Bhanu and Dr. Vineetha Menon supervised the fieldwork and edited the dissertations.

GLOSSARY OF LOCAL TERMS

Aduppu	Hearth
Aduppumannu	The soil used for polishing the hearth
Ambu	Arrow
Ancharp, Cheruppu	A wooden leveller
Asharipura	House made by carpenter
Atakka kathi	Knife used for cutting arecanut
Arival	Sickle
Aru kadavu	Kidnapping and marrying
Attam	Platform on the roof
Changola	Chain designed in a particular shape, made of a mixture of bronze, copper and silver
Chempadam	A broad ring formed by the union of two silver rings, worn on the upper part of the right hand
Chethana	A platform where hearth is located
Churakkai	Bottleguard
Eni	Ladder
Enna	Oil
Kaavala	Anklet
Kadukkan	Traditional & symbolic ear ornament of married male. It is a small ellipse shaped gold ring.

Kaivala	Bangles made of glass or lead
Kakkinam	Feeding shell
Kampivala	A simple trap made of iron wires
Karavala	Bamboo stem used while milking
Kathumara	An oval shaped gold ear-ring worn above the *manikathala*
Kathuminni	Traditional & symbolic ear ornament of unmarried males. It is an oval shaped gold ring with a square shaped disc infront
Kathumullu	Ear ornament- a round ring of gold, worn by unmarried women
Kattapura	Traditional house, made of a peculiar type of *katta* (unbaked mud brick)
Kaylu, Mukki	Ladles made of coconut shell
Keni	Pond
Kokka	Bamboo stick used for threshing paddy
Kol	A tube like artefact made of bamboo
Kolkali, Vattakali	Dances performed at the time of marriage and puberty
Kolai	Small varandha
Komma	Bamboo basket
Komma	Basket made of bamboo splits and smeared with cowdung for storing grains
Koodothram	Sorcery
Koovala kai	A nut
Kortha	Bamboo net
Kudi or *veedu*	Settlement
Kulam	Clan
Kathipakulam *Vadakkekulam* *Villippakulam* Vengadakulam	Clan names
Kula daivam	Clan god

Kunthani	Mortar
Kurikuthuka	Tattooing
Kuthuvala	Nylon net
Kutta, Chada	Bamboo baskets for keeping rice
Kuttikaruthi	Small girl
Kuttikudukka	Mini-pot
Manavalan nayattu	The custom by which a groom is obliged to go hunting, during his first visit to the bride's house
Manikathala / penkathala	Ear ornament, consists of a round gold ring of many beads, worn at the top of the ear by married women.
Mannuvilakku	Lamp-a small plate like structure made of mud.
Manthalam, Mannalam	Bamboo plate for serving food
Manthrica	Chanting
Mattu	Purified clothes
Meenkudu, Kortha	Nets made of bamboo
Meenkutta	Bamboo basket for keeping fish while fishing
Metty	Wooden bar to tie bullocks
Moorthathali	A chain, which is a symbol of married woman, consists of a single round shaped gold ornament known as *tali*
Mudalappura	bamboo house
Mudiyirakkal	Removal of hair
Mukkuthi / Mukkupotte	Nose ornaments
Mukku vazhi	¾ of the way
Muram	Winnow
Muthari	Ragi
Muthy	Wife of the *porunnavan*
Nadu	Sub-division of an area of land owned by its inhabitants
Narikuntham	A wooden pole with an iron spear at one end. It is used to hunt tigers.

Ngengal	Wooden plough
Nilavilakku	Bell metal lamp
Nnjan	Bow-string made of fibre of *manali*, a creeper
Nukam	Wooden horizontal bar
Oi koodal	Running away and then getting married
Pana	Ceiling
Pandal	Temporary shed
Parakolu	An iron stick with a sharp end on one side
Param	Cot made of bamboo
Parambu	Broad and long mat like structure made of reed splits, used for drying grains
Parisapanam	Bride price
Pasha-kolu	A bamboo stick, on top of which gum is pasted for catching birds.
Pathayam	A wooden box fixed in one of the four corners of the single-roomed house for storing grains
Pattavala	Bangles worn around the wrist
Pelat	A square box made of bamboo split used for keeping clothes
Pera	House
Pichathy, kacharakathy,	Sickles/knives of different size and shape *arival, vettukathy* with iron blade and wooden handle
Pittuvirunnu	A bundle of dosa called *pittu* is carried by a bride and is distributed in her settlement during her visit to her natal home, usually on the third day after marriage
Porathavan	Successor of *porunnavan*
Porunnavan	Headman of the settlement

Potha	Lamp-a bamboo stick with a cloth wound at the tip
Prasnam	Divination
Pulikatchu	Soup prepared from mango
Pullu-paya	Grass mat, used for sitting and sleeping
Punnyaham	Holy water
Talachul	The political chieftain of the Mullukurumba, whose control extends over the entire community
Tantri	Priest
Thalakathi, mudikathi	Knives used for cutting hair and shaving face
Thandu	Pestle
Thannikundu	Water container
Thannikundu	A raised platform used for keeping washed vessels and pots filled with water
Theendukulam	Untouchable clans
Theepattam	Extention of the platform of the hearth
Thodare / Arnajanam	Silver thread, waist-band for males
Tholanki	A single hard ring of silver, worn just above the elbow
Thottukali	Touch and run play
Thunakkaran	Guard/Assistant
Uchar	An initiation ceremony performed in connection with hunting
Ury	Swing shelf made of creepers and is used for keeping milk and curd
Valapott kali	Bangle piece game
Valiyapura / Daivapura	A separate, sacred, single-roomed hut, seen in the middle of every settlement
Varantha	Raised platform around the house
Vattakuduma	A traditional hairstyle of men. Knot is made on the hair by keeping it to the left side of the head

Vetu kadavu	Father of the boy takes initiation for the marriage of his son.
Veichapad	Oracle
Vellakaruthi	Lady
Vellinool / Aranjanam	Waist-band of children, made of silver
Vennakkal	Particular stone used for building house
Veri	An implement use to catch birds & squirrels
Villu	Bow
Wayal	Paddy fields

The photographs given in this book were taken by Dr. B. Ananda Bhanu and the figures were drawn by an artist.

BIBLIOGRAPHY

Aiyappan, A. (1936), Blood Groups of the Pre-Dravidians of the Wayanad Plateau. *Man* 36: 255.

Aiyappan, A. (1937), Social and Physical Anthropology of the Nayadis of Malabar. *Bulletin* of the Madras Government Museum 2: (4).

Aiyappan, A. (1948), *Socio-economic Conditions of the Aboriginal Tribes of the Madras Presidency*. Madras: Madras Government Press.

Aiyappan, A. (1965), *Social Revolution in a Kerala Village*. Bombay: Asia Publishing House.

Aiyappan, A. (1982), *The Personality of Kerala*. Trivandram: University of Kerala.

Aiyappan, A. (1988), *Tribal Culture and Tribal Welfare*. Selected Papers by Dr. A. Aiyappan. Edited by U.C. Mohanty. Madras: University of Madras.

Aurora, G.S. (1972), *Tribe-caste-class Encounter*. Hydrabad: Administrative Staff College of India.

Bailey, F.G. (1958), *Caste and the Economic Frontier: A Villagae in Highland Orissa*. Manchester: Manchester University Press.

Bailey, F.G. (1960), *Tribe, Caste and Nation: Study of Political Activity and Political Changes in Highland Orissa*. London: Oxford University Press.

Bailey, F.G. (1961), Tribe and Caste in India, *Contributions to Indian Sociology* 5, pp. 7–19.

Baine, A. (1891), *Census of India*. 1891 Report.

Barnard, Alan. (1992), "Social and Special Boundary Maintenance Among Southern African Hunter-gatherers", in *Mobility and Territoriality*. Edited by Michael J. Casimir and Aparna Rao, pp. 137–152. Oxford: Berg.

Beach, H., Anderson, M., and Aikiop (1992), "Dynamics of Saami Territoriality within the Nation-states of Norway, Sweden and Finland", in *Mobility and Territorialit*. Edited by Michael J. Casimir and Aparna Rao, pp. 137–152. Oxford: Berg.

Bhandari (1980), "The Tribal Situation in India: Industrialization and Urbanisation", in *The Tribal World and it Transformation*. Edited by Bhupinder Singh and J.S. Bhandari, New Delhi: Concept Publishing Company.

Bhanu, B. Ananda (1989), *The Cholanaickan of Kerala*. Calcutta: Anthropological Survey of India. Government of India.

Bhanu, B. Ananda (1999), "Tribal Religion in Kerala", in *Wonder that is Culture*. Edited by T.B. Subba, New Delhi: Mittal Publications.

Bhanu, B. Ananda (2000), "The Tribes of Kerala". *Review Projector (India)*, 3: (1).

Bindu, Ramachandran (2006), Socio-linguistic Interpretation of kinship in an Agricultural Society–a case of Mullukurumba, *The Eastern Anthropologist* 59: (2) pp. 221–227.

Bose, N.K. 1961 (1941), Hindu Method of Tribal Absorption. *Proceedings of Indian Science Congress,* 1941.

Bose, N.K. (1971), *Tribal Life in India*. New Delhi: National Book Trust.

Census of India (1931), Bihar and Orissa, pp. 248–288.

Chatterji, S.K. (1968), *Bolts and Aryan*. Simla: Indian Institute of Advanced Studies.

Chaudhuri, Budhadeb (1992), *Tribal Transformation in India*. Delhi: Inter India Publications.

Dalton, E.T. (1872), *Descriptive Ethnology of Bengal*. Calcutta: Government Press.

Devarapalli, J. (1996), "Ecology and Culture of Chenchus: A Primitive Tribe in Transition", in *Tribal identity in India*. Edited by K.K. Chakravarty, pp. 118–130. Bhopal: Indira Gandhi Rashtriya Manav Sangrahalaya.

Dube, S.C. (1969), "Social Anthropology in India", in *Essays in Memory of D.N. Majumdar*. Edited by T.N. Madan and Gopala Sarana, Bombay: Asia Publishing House.

Ehrenfels, U.R. (1941), *Mother Right in India*. Oxford: Oxford University Press.

Ehrenfels, U.R. (1952), *The Kadars of Cochin*. Madras: University of Madras.

Elwin, Verrier (1955), *Religion of an Indian tribe*. Calcutta: Oxford University Press.

Forde, C. Daryll (1934), *Habitat, Economy and Society*. London: Methuen & Co. Ltd.

Fuchs, Stephen (1973), *The Aboriginal Tribes of India*. New Delhi: Macmillan Co. of India.

Furer-Haimendorf, C. Von (1943), *The Aboriginal Tribes of Hyderabad*. London: Macmillan & Co.

Furer-Haimendorf, C. Von (1943), *The Chenchus: Junglefolk of Deccan*. London: Macmillan & Co.

Furer-Haimendorf, C. Von. 1979. *The Gonds of Andhra Pradesh: Tradition and Change in Indian Tribes*. New Delhi: Vikas Publishing House.

Furer-Haimendorf, C. Von (1985), *The tribes of India: The Struggle for Survival*. New Delhi: Oxford University Press.

Gardiner, A.G. (1972), "The Palleyan", in *Hunters and Gatherers Today*. Edited by M.G. Bicchieri. New York: Holt, Rinehart and Winston.

Ghurye, G.S. (1943), *The Aborigjins–so–called and their future*. Poona: Ghokhale Institute of Politics and Economics.

Ghurye, G.S. 1963 (1959). *The Scheduled Tribes*. Bombay: Popular Prakasan.

Gnanambal, K. (1954), The Kanikkars of Travancore, their Religious and Magical Practices. Calcutta: Anthropological Survey of India, *Bulletin* 3: (2).

Godlier, Maurice (1978), Territoriality and Property in Primitive Society. *Social Science Information* 17: (3) pp. 399–426.

Grigson, W.G. (1931), *Census of India*. 1931, C.P. and Barar Report. Calcutta: Government of India.

Guha, B.S. (1935), The Racial Affinities of the people of India. *Census of India* Simla 1931, 1and 3.

Guha, B.S. (1944), Racial Elements in Indian Population. *Oxford Papers on Indian Affairs* 22. Bombay: Oxford University Press.

Hazra, (1983), *The Kolams of Yeokmal.* Calcutta: Anthropological Survey of India.

Hewitt, F.J. (1988), Paper on the Early History of Northern India. *Journal of the Asiatic Society.*

Hocking, Paul (1965), *Culture Change Among the Badagas: A Community in South India.* Berkeley: California University Press.

Hutton, J.H. (1921), *The sema Nagas.* London: Macmillan and Co. Ltd.

Hutton, J.H. (1921), *The Angami Nagas, with some Notes on the Neighbouring Tribes.* London: Macmillan and Co.

Hutton, J.H. (1923), The Connection of Different Nagas and other Tribes in Assam, *Census of India.* Assam, Shillong 1921, 3. Calcutta: Govt. of India Press.

Hutton, J.H. (1935), *Census of India* 1. Calcutta: Govt. of India Press.

Iyer, L.A. Krishna and L.K. Balaratnam (1948), *The Coorg Tribes and Castes.* Vol. 1, Trivandrum: Government Press.

Iyer, L.A. Krishna (1937), *The Travancore Tribes and Castes.* Vol.1, Trivandrum: Government Press.

Iyer, L.A. Krishna (1939), *The Travancore Tribes and Castes.* Vol. 2, Trivandrum: Government Press.

Iyer, L.A. Krishna (1941), *The Travancore Tribes and Castes.* Vol. 3, Trivandrum: Government Press.

Iyer, L.A. Krishna (1961), *Kerala and her People.* Palghat: The Educational Supplied Depot.

Iyer, L.K. Anantha (1908), *Cochin Tribes and Castes.* Vol. 1. Government of Cochin, London: Higgin Botham and Co.

Iyer, L.K. Anantha (1912), *Cochin Tribes and Castes.* Vol. 2. Government of Cochin, London: Higgin Botham and Co.

Iyer, L.K. Anantha (1928), *The Mysore Tribes and Castes.* Vol. 1. Mysore: Mysore University.

Iyer, L.K. Anantha (1930), *The Mysore Tribes and Castes.* Vol. 3. Mysore: Mysore University.

Iyer, L.K. Anantha (1931), *The Mysore Tribes and Castes.* Vol. 4. Mysore: Mysore University.

Iyer, L.K. Anantha (1935), *The Mysore Tribes and Castes.* Vol. 1. Mysore: Mysore University.

Kosambi, D.D. (1965), *The Culture and Civilization of Ancient India in Historical Perspective.* London: Routledge & Kegan Paul Ltd.

Kulirani, B. Francis (1982), Impact of Cash Crop Economy on the Tribes of Wynad, *Journal of Indian Anthropological Society* 17: 1–12.

Kulirani, B. Francis (1996), "Identity and Integration of the Paniyan of Wayanad", in *Tribal Identity in India.* Edited by K.K. Chakravarty, pp. 162–173. Bhopal: Indira Gandhi Rashtriya Manav Sangrahalaya.

Kurup, K.K.N. (1988), *Modern Kerala: Study in Social & Agrarian Relation.* New Delhi: Mittal Publications.

Lacey, (1931), *Census of India.* 1931 Report, Bihar and Orissa Calcutta: Government of India.

Leuva, K.K. (1964), *The Asur, the Study of Iron Smelters.* New Delhi: Bharathiya Adimjatti Sevak Sangh.

Levi–Strauss, Claude (1963), *Structural Anthropology.* New York: Basic Books.

Levi–Strauss, Claude (1963), *Totemism.* Boston: Beakon Press.

Logan, William 1981 (1887), *Malabar Manual.* No. 1. Trivandrum: Charitram Publications.

Luiz, A.A.D (1962), *Tribes of Kerala.* New Delhi: Bharatiya Adimjati Sevak Sangh.

Majumdar, D.N. 1961 (1958). *Races and cultures of India.* Bombay: Asia Publishing House.

Majumdar, D.N. (1962), *Himalayan Polyandry.* Bombay: Asia Publishing House.

Mandelbaum, David, G. (1938), Polyandry in Kota Society. *American Anthropologist* 40: pp. 574–583.

Mandelbaum, David, G. (1941), Culture Change Among the Nilgiri Tribes. *American Anthropologist* 43.

Mandelbaum, David, G. (1943), "The World and Worldview of the Kota", in *Village India*. Edited by M. Marriot, Chicago: Chicago University Press.

Mandelbaum, David, G. (1970), *Society in India*. Bombay: Asia Publishing House.

Mann, R.S. (1980), *Hakki Pikki: The Trappers and Sellers*. Caucutta: Anthropological Survey of India.

Mathur, P.R.G. (1977), *Tribal Situation in Kerala*. Trivandrum: Historical Society, University of Kerala.

Mencher, Joan, P. (1975), "Anthropological and Sociological Research in Kerala: Past, present and Future Directions", in *Essays on South India*. Edited by Burton Stein, New Delhi: Vikas Publications.

Menon, T. Madhava and M. Sasikumar (1999), *Encyclopaedia of Dravidian Tribes*. Thiruvananthapuram: The International School of Dravidian Linguistics. 1, 2, and 3.

Misra, P.K. (1969), The Jenu Kuruba. Calcutta: Anthropological Survey of India, Government of India, *Bulletin* 18: (3).

Misra, P.K. (1977), "Patterns of Inter-tribal Relations", in *Tribal Heritage of India*. Edited by S.C. Dube, New Delhi: Govt. of India. Ministry of Home Affairs.

Misra, P.K. (1977), "The Jenukurumba", in *Primitive Tribe the first step*. Edited by Surjith Sinha and B.D. Sharma, New Delhi: Vikas Publications.

Morab, S.G. (1977), The Soliga of Biligiri Rengan Hills. Calcutta: Anthropological Survey of India, Government of India. *Memoir* 45.

Morris, Brain (1976), Settlement and Social Change Among the Hill Pandaram, *Man in India* 56 : (2) pp. 134–151.

Morris, Brain (1977), Tappers, Trappers and Hill Pandaram, *Anthropos* 72: pp. 225–241.

Mukherjee, Bhabananda (1953), Socio-economic Organization of the Kanikkar of Travancore. Calcutta: Anthropological Survey of India, Government of India, *Bulletin* 2: (2) pp. 33–82.

Mukherjee, Bhabananda (1954), The Malapantaram of Travancore. Calcutta: Anthropological Survey of India, Government of India, *Bulletin* 3: (1).

Mukherjee, Bhabananda (1956), Marriage Smong the Kanikkar of Travancore. Calcutta: Anthropological Survey of India, Government of India, *Bulletin* 5: (1).

Muller, Max. F. 1988 (1887). *Three Introductory Lectures on the Science of thought.* New Delhi: Asian Education Services.

Nag, M.K. (1954), Family Structure of the Kanikkars of Travancore. Calcutta: Anthropological Survey of India. Government of India, *Bulletin* 3: (3).

Nayak, R. etal. (1990), *The Kondhs–a hand book for Development.* New Delhi: Indian Social Institute.

Netting, Robert (1971) *The Ecological Approaches in Cultural Study.* Philipines: Addison-Wasely Modular Publications.

O' Malley 1906–25. *Bengal District Gazetteers.* Calcutta: Bengal Secretariat Book Depot, 38 Vols.

Oswalt (1976), *An Anthropological Analysis of Food Getting Techniques.* London: John Wiley & Sons.

Pasayath, Chitrasen (1998), *Tribe, Caste and Folk Culture.* New Delhi: Rawat Publications.

Pathy, Jaganath (1987), *Anthropology of Development-Demystification and Relevance.* New Delhi: Gian Publishing House.

Prasad, Maheswari (1980), "Impact of Urbanisation on a Tribal Village: A Case Study of Tusmu Chotanagpur", in *The Tribal World and it Transformation.* Edited by Bhupinder Singh and J.S. Bhandari. New Delhi: Concept Publishing Company.

Radcliffe-brown (1952), *Structure and Function in Primitive Society.* London: Cohen & West.

Raghaviah, V. (1956), *Tribes of India.* New Delhi: Bharatiya Adimjati Sevak Sangh.

Raghaviah, V. (1962), *The Yanadis: A Tribe of Andhra Pradesh.* New Delhi: Bharatiya Adimjati Sevak Sangh.

Rajalakshmi Misra (1971), The Mullkurumba of Kappala. Calcutta: Anthropological Survey of India, Government of India. *Memoir* 30.

Rajalakshmi Misra (1972), Inter-tribal Relations in Erumad. *The Eastern Anthropologist 25*: (2).

Rajendran, P.R. Bhasetkaur and B.V. Bhanu (2003), Fossilized Hominid Baby Skull from the Ferry Crease, Odai, from Bommayar Palayam, Villupuram District of Tamilnadu, South India, *Current Science* 84: (6) pp. 754–756.

Rajendran, P. et al. (2003), Unearthing India's Second Oldest Human Fossil. *Nature*–news India, June p. 7.

Rajendran, P., M.P. Chougankan and C.S.B. Iyer (2004), Human Baby's Skull Fossil within the Middle Pleistocene ferrie crease. Pura tattva, *Bulletin* of Archaeological Society, New Delhi: 24, pp. 1–4.

Rajendran, P., Peter Koshy and Santh Sadasiva (2006), SEM: Study on a Middle Pleistocene Human Skull Fossil. *Soveneer & Abstract* of the National Council on Electron Microscopy and 28th Annual Meeting of Electron Microscope Society of India, p. 16, Thiruvananthapuram: R.R.L.

Rajendran, P. (2006), Studies on a Human Fossil Endomed within a Ferrie Crece. 16th Congress of the International Union for Pre-historic and Protohistoric Sciences. *Book of Abstracts* 1, p. 46. Lisbon.

Ramdas, G. (1925), The Aboriginal Tribes, in *Ramayana* 5.

Rao, Aparna (1992), "The Constrians of Nature of Culture? Pastoral Resources and Territorial behavior in the Western Himalayas", in *Mobility and Territoriality*. Edited by Michael J. Casimir and Aparna Rao, pp. 91–134. Oxford: Berg.

Ray, P.C. (1955), The Manual Ability of the Kanikkar of Trvancore, *Bulletin of the Department of Anthropology* 4: (1) pp. 63–66.

Redfield, Robert (1934), Culture Change in Yucatan. *American Anthropologist* 31, pp. 57–69.

Redfield, Robert (1941), *Folk cultures of Yucat*an.Chicago: University of Chicago Press.

Redfield, Robert (1955), *The Little Community*. Chicago: University of Chicago Press.

Risley, H.H. (1901), *Census of India*, India Report. Calcutta: Govt. of India.

Risley, H.H. (1905), *The people of India*. Calcutta: Secretariat Press.

Rizvi, B.R. (1994), Under the Shadow of Industrialisation-A Study on the Gond of South Central India. *Man and Life* 3 & 5, pp. 209–222.

Rizvi, B.R. (1996), "Ongoing Challenges", in *Tribes in India*. Edited by R.S. Mann. New Delhi: M.A. Publications.

Rivers, W.H.R. (1906), *The Todas*. London: Macmillan & Co. Ltd.

Roy, S.C. (1928), *Oraon Religion and Customs*. Ranchi: Man in India Office.

Sachchidananda (1964), *Culture Change in Tribal Bihar*. Calcutta: Bookland Pvt. Ltd.

Sack, Robert David (1986), *Human Territoriality: Its Theory and History*. Cambridge: Cambridge University Press.

Sahay, K.N. (1962), Trends of Sanskritisation Among the Oraon. *Bulletin of Bihar Tribal Research Institute* 4: (2).

Sahay, K.N. (1968), "Christianity as an Agency of Tribal Welfare in India", in *Applied Anthropology in India. Edited by* L.P. Vidyarthi. Allahabad: Kitab Mahal.

Sahlins, D. Marshal (1965), "Culture and Environment", in *Horizons of Anthroplogy*. Edited by Sol Tax, pp.132–147. *London*: George Allen and Unwin Ltd.

Sahlins, D. Marshal (1972), *Stone Age Economics*. Chicago: Aldine Publishing.

Sasikumar, M. (1997), Tribe–non–tribe Interaction: A Case Study of the Kanikkar of Thiruvananthapuram District. *Ph. D. Thesis* (Unpublished) Submitted to the University of Calicut, Kerala.

Sasikumar, M. (1998), Eco-change and Subsistence Pattern Among Kanikkar of Kerala. *PILC Journal of Dravidic Studies* 8: (1) pp. 69–73.

Sen Gupta, S.K. (1969), *The Portrit of Mahali Economy: The Economic Pattern of Tribal Basketm Makers*. Calcutta: Edition Indiana.

Sharma, B.D. (1976), *Growth Centres in Tribal Areas (Occasional papers on Tribal Development*. 5) New Delhi: Ministry of Home Affairs.

Sherring, M.A. 1975 (1909). *The Tribes and Castes of Madras Presidency, Together with an Account of the Tribes and Castes of Mysore, Nilgiri and Travancore, etc.*, Delhi: Cosmo Publications.

Shoobert (1931), *Census of India*. 1931, C.P. and Barar Report. Calcutta: Govt. of India.

Singh, K.S. (1972), *Tribal Situation in India*. Simla: Indian Institute of Advanced Studies.

Singh, K.S. (1977), Colonial Transformations of Tribal Society in Middle India. *Presidential Address*. Indian History Congress. Bhuvaneshwar.

Singh, K.S. (1999), *People of India. All communities*. 4, 5, 6 Madras: Oxford University Press.

Singh, K.S. (2002), *People of India. Kerala*, 27. Madras: Affiliated East West Press. Pvt. Ltd.

Singh, K.S. (1994), *The Scheduled Tribes*. People of India (National Series, 3). Anthropological Survey of India. New Delhi: Oxford University Press.

Sinha, S.C. (1976), *Anthropology in India*. 1, Calcutta: Anthropological Survey of India.

Sinha, Surajit (1953), Some Aspects of Change in Bhumia Religion in South Manbhum, Bihar, *Man in India* 33: (2).

Sinha, Surajit (1958), Tribal Cultures of Peninsular India as a Dimension of Little Tradition in the Study of Indian Civilization. *Journal of American Folklore* 71, pp. 504–18.

Sinha, Surajit (1959), Bhumij Kshatriya Movements in South Manbhum, *Bulletin of Anthropological Survey of India*. 8: (2).

Sinha, Surajit (1962), State Formation and Rajput myth in Central India. *Man in India* 42: (2).

Sinha, Surajit (1965), Tribe-caste and Tribe-peasant Continuum in Central India. *Man in India* 45 (1) pp. 58–53.

Srivastava (1958), *The Tharu–A Study in Cultural Dynamics*. Agra: Agra University Press.

Tharakan, P.K. Michael (1978), Dimensions and Characteristics of the Migration of Farmers from Travencore to Malabar: 1930–1950. *Journal of Kerala Studies* (Trivandrum). 5: (2) June.

Tharakan, G. and B.A. Bhanu (1994), Tradition and Transition of Culture Among the Mullukurumba of Nilgiri. *PILC Journal of Dravidic Studies*. 4: (1), pp. 95–102.

Thurston, Edgar (1909), *Castes and Tribes of Southern India*. Vol. 11. New Delhi: Cosmo Publications.

Tyagi, Deepak (2002), *People of India. Kerala*. Vol. XXVII. Edited by K.S. Singh. Madras: Affiliated East West Press. Pvt. Ltd.

Verghese, I. (1974), The Kota. Calcutta: Anthropological Survey of India. Government of India. *Bulletin* 18: (2).

Vidyarthi, L.P. (1966), Social Anthropological Researches in India: Some Preliminary Observation. *Journal of Social Research* 9: (1).

Vidyarthi, L.P. (1978), *Rise of Anthropology in India.* 1 & 2. New Delhi: Concept Publishing Company.

Vidyarthi, L.P. and B.K. Rai (1985), *The Tribal Culture of India.* New Delhi: Concept Publishing Company.

Vyas, S.N. (1967), *India in the Ramayana Age.* Delhi: Athma Raj and Sons.

W.G. Lancy *Census of India* 1931, Bihar and Orissa: 248, 288. Calcutta: Govt. of India.

Walker, Anthony Rupert (1986), *The Toda of South India: A New Look.* New Delhi: Hindustan Publishing Company.

Wargo, John (1988), Property Theory of Land use behaviour. *Society and Natural Resources* 1: (2) pp. 189–203.

M.A. Dissertations*

Alakkadan, Satheesan (1990), *Traditional Politcal Organisation among the Mullukurumbas of Nilgiri District.*

Ambalaparambath, Babu (1990), *Land Alienationand Tension Among the Mullukurumbas of Nilgiri District.*

Bindu B. (1990), *Settlement Pattern and House Types of the Mullukurumbas of Nilgiri District.*

Deepthi Mary Jacob (1990), *Child Rearing Practices Among the Mullukurumbas* Nilgiri District.

Harischandran (1990), *Impact of Development Programmes Among the Mullukurumbas of Nilgiri District.*

Jessy Joseph, P. (1990), *Marriage and Family Pattern Among the Mullukurumbas of Nilgiri District.*

Laly Francis (1990), *Religious Practices and Festivals Among the Mullukurumbas* of Nilgiri District.

Leena, P.L. (1990), *Economic Organization.*

Prasanth. (1990), *Health, Disease and Curing Pattern Among the Mullukurumbas of Nilgiri District.*

Premarajan, K. (1990), *Dress and Ornaments among the Mullukurumbas of Nilgiri District.*

Tharakan, George (1990), *Culture Change Among the Mullukurumbas of Nilgiri District.*

Vidya Chandrasekhar (1990), *Food and Food Technologies among the Mullukurumbas of Nilgiri District.*

* *Data collection was made as a part of M.A. Degree in Anthropology in 1990. Dr. B. Ananda Bhanu & Dr. Vineetha Menon supervised the fieldwork and edited the dissertations.*

INDEX